Living

MW01248482

A Practical Guide for Everyday Faith

Table of Contents

Dedication

To my wonderful husband, Ben—my steady place, my
partner, and the calm in every storm.
To my beautiful daughters, Kristen and Madison—you make
my heart burst with pride.
To my amazing sons-in-law, Zach and Rob—you love my
girls well, and for that I'll always be grateful.
To my sweet grandson, Alfie—and every spectacular
grandchild God has yet to bring into my life—you are answers
to prayer and joy in its purest form.

To my parents, Charles and Paulette, and my sister, Christie—
thank you for shaping me, supporting me, and reminding me
what family means.

I love you all deeply. I'm endlessly proud of you. You inspire
me every single day.
I couldn't imagine walking through this life with anyone else
beside me—Thank you for being my people.

You are all God's greatest gifts to me.

Opening Prayer:
"Dear Lord, Please Bless the One Holding This Book (and Maybe Keep Them Awake Through Chapter Six)"

Dear Lord,

Thank You.

Thank You for whoever is holding this book right now—whether they bought it on purpose, borrowed it from a friend, or stumbled across it in a moment of curiosity (or desperation). However it got into their hands, I believe You had something to do with it. Because You're just that good at getting our attention when we need You most.

I don't know what's going on in their life today, but You do. You see all the behind-the-scenes stuff they carry. The weariness, the questions, the "What's the point?" prayers, and even the "I really should read my Bible more but I also just binge-watched three seasons of a baking show" guilt. You see all of it—and You love them completely. Not "once they get it together" love. Right now love.

So, before they turn another page, I want to ask something big (but not too scary): Will You meet them here?

Right here. On this page. In this chair. In the middle of whatever kind of day they're having. I'm not asking for fireworks. Just presence. Gentle, holy presence. The kind that stills the soul and whispers, "Hey, I'm here. And I'm not leaving."

God, in Chapter One, we'll ask: Who are You? That's a bold place to start—but it matters. So I pray this reader comes face-to-face with a deeper understanding of who You are to them personally. Not who their pastor says You are. Not who religion or trauma or Sunday school framed You to be. But the real You. Gracious. Just. Kind. Patient. Holy. Playful. Mighty. Personal. Help them unlearn what's false and rediscover what's always been true.

And Lord, as we roll into Chapter Two and talk about struggle... be gentle. Because the truth is, we all struggle. Even the ones who smile big and serve faithfully and post daily devotionals. We're all walking through something. So help this reader name it—not with shame, but with honesty. Teach them that acknowledging the struggle is not the opposite of faith—it is faith. Because it says, "I trust You enough to be real."

Then in Chapter Three, we'll talk about grace and forgiveness. And honestly, I hope You overwhelm them with it. Wreck them a little (in a good way). Help them realize they don't have to earn what You've already given. That they're not on spiritual probation, waiting for a better version of themselves to be lovable. They are loved. Right now. Grace doesn't come with performance clauses. Thank You for that.

In Chapter Four, we shift to relationship. God, I pray this reader learns what it means to truly know You—not just know about You. Help them talk to You like a friend, not a religious checklist. Teach them how to sit with You in silence and also how to laugh with You while stuck in traffic. Show them that this whole "relationship with God" thing is less about rituals and more about rhythm—a daily, living, breathing connection.

Now, Chapter Five might be my favorite: balancing faith and fun. Because sometimes we act like joy and holiness can't sit at the same table. But You created joy! Laughter! Donuts! Help this reader know it's okay to delight in life. That fun isn't a betrayal of spiritual maturity—it's part of it. Let them laugh loud, rest well, dance freely, and see every good and goofy thing as a gift from You.

Then, Lord, in Chapter Six, we get to the tough stuff: daily habits. I already know what's coming—a bit of conviction, maybe some rolling eyes, and that subtle guilt we all carry for "not doing enough." Please remind them: this isn't about performance. It's about presence. Help them build habits not to get closer to You (You're already right here)—but to notice You more. Give them grace for the days they forget and joy for the days they don't.

Chapter Seven is about triggers—those things that send us spiraling, snapping, or shutting down. I pray for gentleness here, Lord. Help them recognize what keeps pulling them off course without falling into shame. Whether it's insecurity, stress, isolation, or Taco Bell at 10 p.m.—reveal what's going on beneath the surface. And then, gently, start healing it.

Chapter Eight dives into temptation—and You know how sneaky that can be. So give them eyes to see it, strength to resist it, and humility to ask for help. Whether the temptation is sin, distraction, self-sabotage, or the lie that they're too far gone—remind them that there's always a way out. That grace doesn't expire. That You're not disappointed— they're invited to walk in freedom.

Next comes Chapter Nine: community. And oh boy, that's a tricky one. I pray You bring the right people into this reader's life—people who love You, love them, and aren't scared off by their quirks. I pray they find a church family where they don't have to fake it, a friend who checks in just because, and a safe space to grow. And Lord? If this reader is introverted, like me, awkward, also like me, or recovering from church hurt—give them courage. Heal what was broken and restore what was missing.

Then, Chapter Ten: embracing imperfection. Deep breath, God. Because that's hard. We're all so used to striving, editing, curating, comparing. Help this reader realize that You're not asking them to be flawless. You're asking them to be faithful. That You work through imperfection—not in spite of it. And that they are not a project to fix, but a masterpiece in progress.

In Chapter Eleven, help them see how they can reflect Your love in daily life. Not by preaching in the streets (unless You're calling them to, in which case... wow), but in simple, sacred, quiet ways: a kind word, a patient response, a prayer whispered while doing dishes. Let their life preach louder than any platform ever could.

Finally, Chapter Twelve. Celebrating the journey. God, help them stop long enough to look back and say, "Wow. Look what God has done." Help them not just power through, but praise through. Show them that every small step of obedience, every quiet act of trust, every little breakthrough—it's worth celebrating. Because You've been faithful every step of the way.

And for those bonus reading plans and journaling prompts? I pray they're not just tasks—but tools. May this book not just be something they finish, but something that marks a new beginning.

So Lord, I lift up this reader to You. Cover them with peace. Surprise them with joy. Wreck them with grace. Walk with them as they read. Speak through every chapter, every word, every awkward, scribbled journal line. Meet them in their questions. Hug them in their tears. Nudge them when they try to quit. And remind them, every day, that they are known, loved, and never alone.

Thank You for letting me write this. And thank You for the person reading it.

In Jesus' name,
 Amen.

Introduction

"I Love Jesus, But My Wi-Fi Hates Me"

Last Saturday started off with me boldly declaring: "Today, I will walk in faith, be productive, and drink water like a responsible adult."

That lasted until about 8:17 a.m.

I had just settled in with my Bible and a hot cup of tea, ready for a quiet time that didn't involve distractions, and right on cue, my neighbor decided it was the perfect time to start what I can only assume was chainsaw practice in their driveway. I don't know what they were cutting, but based on the noise, it may have been the Ark of the Covenant.

I tried to ignore it. I even put on my headphones and played instrumental worship music—because surely you can't lose your temper while listening to a pan flute version of Oceans, right?

Wrong.

The chainsaw was soon joined by a lawn mower, two semi trucks racing down the road, and a delivery guy who rang the doorbell like he was in the 4x100 relay. By the time I made it to the door, he had vanished like Elijah in a chariot of Amazon Prime.

And of course, the package wasn't even mine.

Back inside, I opened my laptop to start "weekend" work. Sometimes I pull reports from home, which sounds peaceful until your Wi-Fi starts acting like it's powered by prayer and hamster wheels. Right as I was downloading a file to my laptop, the screen froze, then blinked, then just sighed in defeat like it too had given up on productivity.

I whispered, "Jesus, take the router."

Now I'm not saying I panicked, but I did lay hands on the modem and pray out loud. Nothing happened, except another semi came howling by while the cat cried for food. Probably in tongues. Hard to say.

With the internet still down, I decided to clean my kitchen, because cleanliness is next to godliness—or at least next to procrastination. I pulled out a Tupperware container from the back of the fridge that had become a biological experiment. I have no idea what it used to be, but it now had mold that looked like it had a savings account and long-term goals.

While I was gagging over the sink, my phone buzzed—a text from a friend: "Hey, can you pray for me today? My kid is sick."

I stared at it. I love the Lord. I love my friends. But I also love not panicking over scripture while pretending I didn't just fish out a radioactive casserole. I texted back: "Of course! God's strength is made perfect in weakness. Which is convenient because I am very, very weak."

Later that evening, as I logged onto my laptop for Bible study (with the Wi-Fi now miraculously healed—praise be), While reading I envisioned all the beautiful faces of my family, each one smiling, tired, hopeful, stressed. I stumbled through some verses in Romans. Something about perseverance that I interpreted as sounding more like patience with calluses. I nodded, then teared up. It was messy. And holy.

And that's the thing.

Life isn't some shiny devotional with pastel highlights and sunbeams of clarity. It's burned toast, slow Wi-Fi, someone else's package on your porch, and moldy leftovers. It's tired prayers and imperfect Bible studies and laughing so you don't cry at the chaos of being a grown adult who still doesn't have it all together.

But God is there—in the dropped connections, in the overstimulated nerves, in the moments when we're just trying not to throw our laptops across the room. He's patient. He's present. And thankfully, He doesn't require perfect people to do His perfect work.

So, no—I didn't crush Saturday. But I survived it. With grace, duct tape, and a slightly warmed cup of microwaved tea.

Which, honestly, feels like a win.

I believe deeply in the power of God's grace and the importance of living a life that honors Him. The purpose of this book is to help everyday people, like you and me, grow closer to God without losing the joy of living life fully. Our faith is not about being perfect but about walking daily with the Lord, even amidst life's messiness and struggles.

Life is full of challenges. Balancing faith with the struggles of temptation and worldly desires isn't easy. Many of us are trying to honor God while dealing with frustrations, setbacks, and the distractions of a busy life. I'm not a perfect person—far from it. Like most, I've had unfulfilling jobs, family challenges that weigh on my heart, faced challenging health issues, people who have hurt me, a busy life that leaves little time for doing the things I love, and the everyday frustrations that come with trying to keep it all together. I struggle daily to find meaning in the challenges and to not let my frustrations bubble over.

As I've walked through these struggles, I've learned that faith is not about having all the answers or living without flaws. It's about trusting in a God who loves us unconditionally, even when we fall short. This truth has carried me through my hardest days. There are moments when it feels like everything is crumbling around me, and yet, in those moments, God's presence has been a source of comfort and strength. It's not about avoiding struggles but about finding His purpose and peace in the midst of them.

This book is an invitation to discover how you can grow closer to God while still living a full and joyful life. It's for those who sometimes feel they don't measure up or worry that their imperfections disqualify them from God's love. It's for those who want to experience life to the fullest while honoring God in their choices and actions. We'll explore together how to balance the call to live a holy life with the reality of being human—a balance that is only possible through God's grace.

I've often heard people say they feel disconnected from God because they don't fit the mold of a "perfect" Christian. Perhaps they think they're too flawed, or they feel their struggles with temptation make them unworthy. If that sounds familiar, this book is for you. Let's dispel the myth that following God means living a rigid, joyless life. Instead, let's embrace the truth that God created us to live abundantly and in relationship with Him. He knows our hearts, our desires, and our struggles. And He meets us where we are, offering forgiveness, love, and guidance.

Through the chapters ahead, I'll share practical ways to strengthen your relationship with God, navigate temptation, and find joy in your spiritual journey. We'll talk about what it means to live authentically as a follower of Christ without sacrificing the beauty and excitement of life. Most importantly, we'll explore how to rely on God's grace to overcome life's challenges, find purpose in your struggles, and draw closer to Him every step of the way.

So, if you've ever felt like you're not quite "good enough" for God, let me assure you: He loves you as you are, and He wants to walk with you on this journey. Let's dive in together and discover how to live fully while loving God with all our hearts.

So go ahead and get yourself a journal. Yep, I said it. Buy the pretty one. The one with the gold edges and the inspirational quote on the front that makes you feel like you have your life together, even though you just ate ice cream for dinner again.

Spoiler alert: *You're gonna need it. Not just for deep spiritual insights or tear-soaked repentance letters to Jesus (though those will happen), but also to track all the hilarious ways God works in your life—like that one time you prayed for patience and He sent you a toddler with a kazoo.*

Trust me. This journey? It's going to be messy, beautiful, convicting, and wildly funny. And you'll want receipts.

Part 1: Understanding God and Ourselves

Chapter 1: Who Is God to You?

Opening Prayer:

Dear God, Let's kick this off with a big question—and I pray the reader doesn't immediately panic or Google "safe Christian answers." Help them not feel like they need a theological degree to answer who You are to them. Just meet them where they are. Whether they call You Father, Friend, or "The Mysterious Voice I Hear When I Don't Hit Snooze," speak to their heart. Show them You're real, personal, and not just a cosmic manager with a clipboard. Let this chapter be a holy "aha!" moment—and maybe give them a snack while they read. Amen.

"God Is Not Your Grumpy Vice-Principal"

When I was younger, I thought God was a lot like my middle school vice-principal, tall, stern, always lurking just around the corner waiting to bust you for chewing gum or running in the halls. He didn't smile. Ever. He once threatened me with detention for laughing during an assembly, which, to be fair, was about fire safety and did include an actor in a giant flame costume who tripped on his own foot and fell off the stage. The flame was fine!

But that's beside the point.

What I'm saying is, for a long time, I carried that "God-as-Vice-Principle" idea into my adult faith. I was convinced He was watching me 24/7—not in a warm, "I know the number of hairs on your head" kind of way—but more like, "I'm keeping a tally of every sarcastic comment, every eye roll, and every time you skipped your morning devotional to scroll Instagram."

It got to the point that every time I lost my car keys, stubbed my toe, or got stuck behind someone paying in pennies at the gas station, I'd mutter, "Okay, Lord, I get it. I deserve this. I didn't say grace over those tacos yesterday."19

I lived in spiritual anxiety, constantly trying to earn grace like it was some cosmic credit score. Read my Bible? +10. Thought a rude thought in traffic? -15. Donated to charity? +20. Secretly judged someone's socks in church? -50. That kind of theology will make you spiritually exhausted—and very quiet during altar calls.

One morning, after a particularly rough week (which included a spilled spaghetti on white carpet in an apartment I rented, a forgotten dentist appointment, and a text from my mom asking if I was "still going to church like a good Christian"), I sat down with my Bible, fully expecting to get spiritually whacked upside the head.

I opened to the book of Luke—because I figured if I was about to get convicted, I might as well let Jesus do it gently. That's when I read the parable of the prodigal son.

Now, I know, I know—we've all heard that story a hundred times. But this time, something hit me.

You know the part where the son finally comes to his senses, rehearses his apology speech, and drags himself home expecting to be met with lectures and a job application for stable boy?

But instead—instead—his father sees him from a long way off, runs to him (like a sprint, robe flapping, sandals slapping situation), throws his arms around him, and throws a party with steak.

And for the first time, it occurred to me: This is what God is actually like.

Not a Vice-Principal.

Not a cosmic IRS agent.

Not a joyless taskmaster handing out punishment slips from a celestial clipboard.

He's a Father who celebrates the return, not the mistakes. He's not standing at the door with a list of what I've done wrong—He's already on the porch with open arms and a party playlist.

This was an absolute revelation to me. And like most revelations, I immediately tried to test it in the real world.

So, naturally, the next time I royally messed up—I'm talking "accidentally hit reply-all on an email rant about a coworker (ironically, an IRS agent)" kind of mess up—I didn't spiral into my usual pit of guilt and bargain-praying.

Instead, I paused, took a deep breath, and said out loud: "God, I messed up. And You're probably shaking Your head and laughing, but You still love me. Help me fix this, and maybe keep me from getting fired."

Then I took a large dose of liquid caffeine and fixed my email settings.

Guess what? The world didn't end. My coworker forgave me. And I didn't feel like I needed to atone by fasting for 40 days and sewing blankets for orphans. I just... accepted grace.

What a concept.

The more I've leaned into who God actually is—not the caricature I built in my head—the more peace I've found. Not because my life is now magically issue-free (please see: car battery, dead, twice), but because I finally trust that God isn't waiting to punish me. He's waiting to love me through it.

I still get it wrong. I still catch myself thinking, "God's probably done with me after that one." But then I remember: He knew every boneheaded thing I'd do before I ever took a breath—and He signed up for this relationship anyway.

That kind of love will wreck you—in the best way.

So if you're carrying around a picture of God as your disapproving middle school vice-principal, grumpy judge, or some heavenly version of a passive-aggressive HOA board, can I lovingly suggest you chuck that image straight into the spiritual recycling bin?

Because the God of Scripture—the real God—is not in the business of intimidation. He's in the business of invitation.

Come home. The porch light is on. The party's waiting. And no, He's not mad you forgot your Bible for a week. He's just glad you came back.

Also, He probably thinks that story about the guy in the fire suit falling off the stage is hilarious. He did invent humor, after all.

One of the first steps in drawing closer to God is understanding who He truly is. It's easy to develop misconceptions about God, and these misunderstandings can create barriers to faith and hinder a genuine relationship with Him. Let's begin by addressing these misconceptions and exploring the truth about God's nature.

For many, God is seen as distant, a strict enforcer of rules, or someone who is impossible to please. Others might view Him as a last resort, someone they turn to only in times of crisis. These views often stem from personal experiences, cultural influences, or even misunderstandings of scripture. But the Bible paints a far different picture of God. He is not a taskmaster waiting for us to fail but a loving Father who desires a personal relationship with each of us.

One of the most profound truths about God is found in 1 John 4:8: "Whoever does not love does not know God, because God is love." This verse reminds us that God's very essence is love. It's not just something He does; it's who He is. His love is unconditional, steadfast, and unchanging. Romans 5:8 further illustrates this by saying, "But God demonstrates his own love for us in this: While we were still sinners, Christ died for us." This is the heart of the gospel. God's love is not based on our performance or worthiness; it's a gift freely given.

Despite knowing this truth intellectually, many of us struggle to accept it in our hearts. We might feel unworthy because of our sins or failures. I've been there—feeling like I've let God down too many times to deserve His love. But here's the beautiful thing: God's love isn't something we earn; it's something we receive.

Imagine God's love as the sun. The sun shines regardless of whether we're standing in its light or hiding in the shade. It's constant and unwavering. Similarly, God's love is always there, even when we feel unworthy or distant from Him. Our job is to step into His light and let it transform us.

Understanding who God is also means recognizing His forgiveness. Psalm 103:12 tells us, "as far as the east is from the west, so far has he removed our transgressions from us." When we confess our sins and seek His forgiveness, He wipes our slate clean. This is a truth that can be hard to grasp, especially when we're weighed down by guilt or shame. But God's forgiveness is complete and final. He doesn't hold our past mistakes against us; instead, He invites us to start fresh.

Another important aspect of God's nature is His faithfulness. Deuteronomy 31:6 says, "Be strong and courageous. Do not be afraid or terrified because of them, for the Lord your God goes with you; he will never leave you nor forsake you." In a world where people and circumstances can let us down, God's faithfulness is a rock we can cling to. He is always present, always listening, and always ready to guide us.

In my own life, I've seen God's faithfulness time and time again. There have been moments when I've felt utterly lost, unsure of how to move forward. But in those moments, I've experienced God's gentle guidance, often through prayer, scripture, or the encouragement of others. One example that stands out is a particularly difficult season in my career. I felt stuck, undervalued, and unsure of my purpose. As I prayed and sought God's direction, I began to see doors open that I hadn't noticed before. It wasn't an instant fix, but it was a reminder that God was with me, even in the struggle.

God's role in our lives is also deeply personal. He isn't just the Creator of the universe; He is intimately involved in the details of our lives. Jesus says in Matthew 10:30, "And even the very hairs of your head are all numbered." This level of care and attention is almost unimaginable, yet it's a testament to how much God values each of us.

Consider the story of Hagar in Genesis 16. Alone and desperate in the wilderness, she encounters God, who sees her pain and speaks directly to her situation. Overwhelmed, she calls Him El Roi, "the God who sees me." This moment reveals that even in our lowest and most hidden places, God is present, attentive, and deeply compassionate. Just like Hagar, we can be assured that God sees us, knows us, and cares personally about our journey.

Yet, understanding God also means wrestling with our struggles and doubts. Sometimes, we face moments of questioning: "Is God really with me?" or "Why would He care about someone like me?" These doubts are not uncommon, and the Bible is full of individuals who wrestled with God in similar ways. Consider the story of Job, a man who lost everything yet ultimately discovered the depth of God's sovereignty and faithfulness. Job's journey wasn't about getting easy answers; it was about coming to a place of trust and reverence for God, even in the face of suffering.

Psalm 34:18 reminds us, "The Lord is close to the brokenhearted and saves those who are crushed in spirit." This verse highlights an essential aspect of God's character: His nearness. He is not a distant deity observing us from afar; He is Emmanuel, "God with us." He walks with us through our struggles, offering comfort and strength.

As we navigate the challenges of life, it's crucial to remember that God's love is transformative. It's not a passive force but an active one that reshapes our hearts and minds. Romans 12:2 urges us, "Do not conform to the pattern of this world, but be transformed by the renewing of your mind. Then you will be able to test and approve what God's will is—his good, pleasing, and perfect will." This transformation isn't about becoming perfect overnight. It's a lifelong journey of growth, surrender, and trust.

So, who is God to you? Is He a distant figure, a stern judge, or a loving Father? Reflect on your own experiences and beliefs. If you've been holding onto misconceptions about God, I encourage you to lay them down and seek Him anew. Open your Bible, spend time in prayer, and ask Him to reveal His true nature to you.

Understanding who God is requires more than just theological knowledge; it demands a personal encounter. King David, in Psalm 27:4, expressed his longing to know God intimately: "One thing I ask from the Lord, this only do I seek: that I may dwell in the house of the Lord all the days of my life, to gaze on the beauty of the Lord and to seek him in his temple." This heart cry captures the essence of a relationship with God. It's not about rules or rituals but about seeking His presence and delighting in who He is.

Moreover, our understanding of God should inspire us to worship Him. Worship is not confined to singing hymns or attending church services; it's a lifestyle of honoring God in all we do. Romans 11:36 reminds us, "For from Him and through Him and for Him are all things. To Him be the glory forever! Amen." When we recognize God as the source and purpose of our lives, worship becomes a natural response.

Finally, let's consider the role of community in understanding God. Fellowship and accountability are vital in the Christian walk. Proverbs 27:17 says, "As iron sharpens iron, so one person sharpens another." Surrounding ourselves with fellow believers helps us grow in our faith and provides opportunities to witness God's love in action. Your first step to getting closer to God should be surrounding yourself and getting plugged into relationships with other Christians. Whether that be at church, a coffee group, or just even one Godly friend who will commit to encouraging you to grow. If you don't belong to a Bible-believing church, I encourage you to find one—one that loves unconditionally and one where you can relate and grow. Community plays a vital role in deepening our relationship with God and offers a safe space to share struggles, celebrate victories, and grow together in faith.

In closing, let's keep this foundational truth in mind: God is love. He is for you, not against you. He wants a relationship with you, not because you're perfect but because you're His. And in that relationship, you'll find the strength to overcome struggles, the grace to navigate temptations, and the joy of living a life that honors Him. This journey is not about perfection but about connection—a connection to the God who knows you, loves you, and walks with you every step of the way. Embrace this truth, and let it transform how you see yourself, others, and the God who calls you His own.

Closing Prayer:

Well Lord, That was a lot to think about. Thank You for whatever clarity, confusion, or curiosity this chapter stirred up. Whether the reader finished with a neatly labeled identity for You or just a hunger to know You more—that's a win. Keep showing up in unexpected ways (even if it's through burnt toast or toddler tantrums). Amen.

Chapter 2: Acknowledge the Struggle: Navigating Temptation and Embracing God's Redemption

Opening Prayer:

God, Here we go. This chapter might get uncomfortable. Please help the reader resist the urge to skip ahead to something "more encouraging." Give them courage to face what they usually stuff down with busyness or carbs. Remind them that admitting struggle isn't weakness—it's honesty. And You can work with honest. Help them see You aren't shocked, disappointed, or about to revoke their Christian card. You're just present. And that's enough. Amen.

The Reality of Temptation and the Universal Nature of Sin

Temptation is something that touches every human life, regardless of age, background, or stage of spiritual maturity. It is woven into the very fabric of our human experience. As the Bible states, "all have sinned and fall short of the glory of God" (Romans 3:23), making it clear that sin is not reserved for a specific group but is a shared challenge for all people. Sin manifests in a multitude of ways, sometimes overtly, through actions such as theft or violence, but more often, it takes root in more subtle and less conspicuous forms like thoughts, emotions, and everyday choices that seem harmless but are far from it.

Temptation is the persistent pull toward choosing what is contrary to God's will. The struggles we face in resisting temptation are often more than mere moral battles; they reflect the deep human desire to control our lives, to satisfy immediate desires, or to seek comfort in ways that God never intended. Temptation can feel overwhelming at times because it taps into our desires, weaknesses, and fears. Yet, as pervasive as temptation is, it also highlights the mercy of God — for in recognizing our own shortcomings, we also open ourselves to receive His grace, which is always greater than our sin.

The Bible's acknowledgment of human sinfulness does not leave us in despair. Instead, it invites us into the freedom of God's grace, where even the most common and subtle temptations can be overcome through Christ. We are reminded that no temptation is unique or unprecedented. The apostle Paul reassures us in 1 Corinthians 10:13, "No temptation has overtaken you except what is common to mankind. And God is faithful; he will not let you be tempted beyond what you can bear." This universal nature of sin and temptation invites us into a collective struggle, one where none of us are alone in our fight, and where God's grace makes a way of escape.

Temptation to Gossip

Gossip may seem like a small or trivial temptation, but its impact is far-reaching. It is one of the most common sins that we may encounter in our everyday lives, and one that often masquerades as harmless conversation or social bonding. However, the reality is that gossip, whether it is about someone's character, their actions, or their life circumstances, can have destructive consequences on relationships, communities, and our own spiritual health.

The lure of gossip often lies in the feeling of superiority it gives us. By sharing information — even if it's only partially true or taken out of context — we can elevate ourselves in comparison to the person we're speaking about. It can create a false sense of belonging or importance within a group, as though we have exclusive knowledge or insight. Unfortunately, the temporary satisfaction we gain from gossip often leaves behind lasting damage. The Bible warns us, "A perverse person stirs up conflict, and a gossip separates close friends" (Proverbs 16:28). Gossip erodes trust, destroys relationships, and fosters division. The person being talked about is often harmed by the spread of private details or rumors, and even those participating in gossip are left with a sense of guilt and disunity.

We may justify gossip with rationalizations like, "I'm just venting," or "I'm just sharing information." But these justifications don't negate the harm done. God sees our words as powerful tools that can either build others up or tear them down. As Jesus said in Matthew 12:36, "But I tell you that everyone will have to give account on the day of judgment for every empty word they have spoken." The temptation to gossip is, therefore, not just about engaging in conversation, but about the kind of influence we wield through our words.

When we gossip, we fail to reflect God's call to love our neighbors as ourselves (Matthew 22:39). Instead of showing empathy, we engage in behavior that harms others for our own benefit. Overcoming the temptation of gossip requires a commitment to speaking truth in love, exercising discretion, and promoting peace, not division. The words we speak can either be a balm for wounds or an infection that spreads bitterness. By guarding our tongues and praying for wisdom in our conversations, we align ourselves with God's call to unity and love.

Temptation to Be Lazy

Laziness is a more insidious temptation, one that can slowly take root in our lives without us even realizing it. It's easy to slip into the habit of procrastination or to become complacent in our responsibilities, particularly in a world full of distractions. Whether it's scrolling through social media for hours, binge-watching television shows, or simply avoiding difficult tasks, the temptation to be lazy often manifests when we seek comfort over discipline or relaxation over responsibility.

In the book of Proverbs, laziness is linked with a lack of wisdom and foresight. Proverbs 6:9-11 warns, "How long will you lie there, you sluggard? When will you get up from your sleep? A little sleep, a little slumber, a little folding of the hands to rest — and poverty will come on you like a thief and scarcity like an armed man." Laziness, when unchecked, leads not only to a failure to complete tasks but also to a deeper erosion of character and purpose.

The root of laziness often lies in a deeper spiritual struggle — a lack of motivation to fulfill the purposes God has set before us. When we allow laziness to dominate, we are rejecting the good work that God has entrusted to us. The Bible calls us to be diligent in all things, working heartily as though for the Lord (Colossians 3:23). Whether it's the work we do in our careers, in our families, or in our personal growth, each task is an opportunity to honor God with our time and effort.

Overcoming the temptation of laziness requires a mindset shift — from seeking comfort and ease to seeking purpose and discipline. It means setting aside distractions, managing our time effectively, and prioritizing tasks that align with God's will for our lives. As we develop a strong work ethic, we reflect the diligence of Christ, who worked tirelessly in His mission on earth. And when we work for God, we remember that the work itself, no matter how mundane, is sacred.

Temptation Not to Pray for Those Who Hurt You

One of the most difficult temptations we face in our lives is the temptation to withhold forgiveness and to refuse to pray for those who have hurt us. Our natural inclination is to hold on to anger, bitterness, and resentment, believing that these emotions somehow give us control or justice. The temptation is to think, "They don't deserve my prayers," or "I'm not ready to forgive them." These feelings are natural, and yet they are at odds with the heart of the Gospel.

Jesus commands us in Matthew 5:44 to love our enemies and pray for those who persecute us. This is not an easy command, and it requires a radical shift in how we view those who have wronged us. When we hold on to anger and refuse to pray for those who have hurt us, we are ultimately only hurting ourselves. Unforgiveness chains us to the past and keeps us trapped in cycles of bitterness and resentment.

Forgiveness doesn't mean excusing the wrong, and it doesn't mean that we instantly feel healed from the pain. Rather, it means choosing to release the hold that the hurt has on us, trusting that God will bring justice in His perfect timing. When we pray for those who have hurt us, we align ourselves with God's will and open the door for His grace to heal and transform our hearts. This act of obedience does not minimize our hurt, but it allows us to reflect the grace that God extends to us daily.

Envy and Pride: The Roots of Many Temptations

Envy and pride are twin temptations that are deeply rooted in the human condition. Envy arises when we compare ourselves to others and feel dissatisfied with what we have. We might look at someone else's success, wealth, or status and feel that we deserve what they have, or worse, that we are somehow less than they are. This discontent leads us to ignore the blessings that God has already given us, focusing instead on what we don't have.

Pride, on the other hand, is the opposite temptation. It tells us that we are better than others, that we can rely on our own strength and intellect, and that we don't need God. It manifests in self-reliance, self-importance, and a refusal to humble ourselves before others. Both envy and pride are destructive because they pull us away from God's truth and make us focus on our own perceived value, rather than recognizing our worth in God.

In the Bible, we see both of these temptations at work. Cain's envy of Abel led to the first murder (Genesis 4:3-8). King Saul's pride drove him to jealousy and fear of David, leading to his downfall (1 Samuel 18-19). Envy and pride distort our understanding of our place in the world and our relationship with others. The antidote to both is humility — the willingness to acknowledge that all we have comes from God, and that we are called to serve, not be served.

When we experience envy or pride, we are invited to turn our hearts toward gratitude, recognizing the good gifts that God has given us. We are also called to celebrate the success of others rather than feeling threatened by it. Through humility, we embrace our dependence on God and our identity as His beloved children, free from the need to compare ourselves to others.

Indulgence: The Temptation to Overconsume

"The Cookie Incident: A True Story of Temptation, Shame, and Chocolate Chips"

Let me start by saying this: I love Jesus. I really do.

But I also really, really love cookies.

And this is how I learned that temptation doesn't always come in the form of dramatic movie moments or wild moral crossroads—it sometimes shows up warm, gooey, and staring at you from a Tupperware container with demonic levels of aroma.

It all started at our Wednesday night small group, which, despite the name, had grown to the size of a minor family reunion. We had been going through a study on Romans, and that week's topic? Temptation and sin.

Perfect.

Sister Margie, a sweet woman in her 60s with the spiritual discernment of a prophet and the baking skills of a Food Network finalist, showed up that night with a tray of homemade chocolate chip cookies. Not just any cookies—no, these were soft in the middle, crisp on the edges, still slightly warm, with little flakes of sea salt on top like she had personally consulted an angel about balance and flavor.

Now, I had already declared—loudly and confidently—that I was on a sugar fast.

"This is my week to detox from sugar and processed foods," I had told the group earlier, while holding a sad little container of raw almonds and what I think was a date that had seen better days. "Temptation comes in many forms, and I'm choosing to rise above it."

Everyone nodded. It was all very holy.

And then Sister Margie walked in with that tray.

The air shifted. The room got quiet. Someone actually said, "Behold, the glory of the Lord," and I'm not entirely sure they were joking.

Now, here's where things go off the rails.

I sat across the room from the cookie tray. Far enough that I couldn't smell them (as long as I breathed through my mouth), but close enough to see the chocolate melting just a little on top.

"No big deal," I thought. "I've got this. I'm spiritually mature. I'm basically fasting for righteousness."

But somewhere between verse six and Paul's explanation of sin's grip on the flesh, I found myself casually getting up to "stretch." You know, just a little arm rotation... walk past the coffee table... maybe look at the cookies... no big deal.

Then someone asked a question, which meant I had to sit back down, still cookie-less. So I did what any red-blooded believer trying to avoid sin does: I started praying.

"Lord," I whispered, "give me the strength to overcome this temptation. Guard my heart. Guard my tastebuds."

But then my brain betrayed me.

What if Sister Margie never makes these again? What if she gets raptured before next week? What if this is your LAST chance to experience this cookie?

I rebuked those thoughts. I did. But I also suddenly needed to "check my phone" near the cookie tray. Which, I admit, was still off in my coat pocket across the room.

I got up. Again.

And then—it happened.

I don't even remember the full decision-making process. All I know is that one moment I was reciting Romans 7:19, and the next, I had a cookie in my hand and was breaking it in half to "share" with someone (no one asked me to). I popped half of it in my mouth like a criminal disposing of evidence.

And y'all... I saw the face of God in that cookie.

It was perfect. Chewy. Sweet. Slightly sinful.

I chewed quickly, making sure no one noticed. But I forgot two things:

1. *We were sitting in a circle.*

2. *Margie was watching.*

She didn't say a word. She just smiled.

I sat back down and tried to focus on the discussion. "The temptations of the flesh," our leader was saying. "They come subtly, disguised as small compromises..."

Was he looking at me? Did he know?

Then I did the most unholy thing of the night: I got up and ate the other half.

Not for nourishment. Not even out of rebellion. Pure, unfiltered cookie lust.

After the study, I stayed to help clean up, mostly so no one would hear my soul crying. As I tossed paper plates and folded chairs, Margie walked over, put a container of cookies in my hand, and whispered, "You can have the rest. Just... maybe don't tell the almonds."

I blushed so hard I almost combusted.

Later that night, sitting on my couch with that cursed blessing of a container in my lap, I opened my Bible again—mostly out of guilt— and reread Romans 3:23: "For all have sinned and fall short of the glory of God."

All.

Even me.

Even with a cookie in my mouth.

The thing is, that verse doesn't say some have sinned. It doesn't say "people who eat the last cookie" or "folks who break their sugar fast." It says all. We've all fallen short.

And while it's funny to joke about sugar fasts and baked goods, the truth is that temptation hits every one of us—daily, hourly, sometimes by the minute. Whether it's food, gossip, jealousy, self-righteousness, anger, or the "justified" snap judgment we make about someone's weird worship face—temptation is part of the human package.

But here's the beauty of it: falling into temptation doesn't mean God's done with us.

He doesn't toss us aside when we mess up. He doesn't wave a divine finger and say, "Well, guess we're done here. You had one job—avoid the cookie." No, He meets us there. In the chocolate crumbs and the shame and the ridiculousness of it all, and He says: "Yeah, you fell short. But I've already paid for that. Let's get back up and keep walking."

So the next time temptation sneaks up in your life—whether it's a big thing or something as dumb as a cookie—just remember: God's not surprised. He already knows. And He loves you still.

But maybe... don't sit directly across from the cookies next time.

Indulgence is another common temptation in our culture of excess. We are surrounded by constant opportunities to overconsume — whether it's food, entertainment, or material possessions. The temptation to indulge can often feel like a temporary escape from stress, pain, or boredom. We might overeat when we're stressed, shop excessively when we're lonely, or binge-watch shows to numb our emotional pain. These indulgences promise relief but often leave us feeling empty afterward.

The Bible warns against overindulgence in 1 Corinthians 6:12, where Paul writes, "I have the right to do anything," you say — but not everything is beneficial. "I have the right to do anything" — but I will not be mastered by anything." Indulgence ultimately leads to addiction, idleness, and a lack of self-control. What we think will fill the emptiness only deepens it, leading us into cycles of consumption that take us further from God's intended purpose for our lives.

Instead of indulging in temporary comforts, God calls us to find satisfaction in Him. We are reminded that He is the source of true peace and joy, and that material things cannot fill the deep longing in our hearts. When we resist the temptation to indulge, we free ourselves from the mastery of cravings and open ourselves to the lasting fulfillment that comes from a relationship with God.

The Temptation to Put Our Own Needs Above Others

One of the most common and powerful temptations we face is the urge to prioritize our own needs, desires, and comfort above those of others. This is especially prevalent in a world that often values individualism and self-sufficiency, where "looking out for number one" is seen as a natural part of achieving success and happiness. However, this mindset can easily become selfishness, and in its most destructive form, it can lead to the disregard of the needs and well-being of those around us.

The temptation to place ourselves first is subtle and sometimes even justified by our own internal narrative. We might say to ourselves, "I need this for my own peace of mind," or "I've worked hard; I deserve a break." There's nothing inherently wrong with taking care of ourselves or setting boundaries, but when self-care becomes self-centeredness, we cross a line.

At its core, this temptation is about control — controlling our time, our resources, and our relationships in such a way that we are the primary focus. It's an easy trap to fall into, especially when we're faced with our own struggles, exhaustion, or the pressures of daily life. Putting others' needs aside may seem like an understandable choice when we're overwhelmed, but it can also prevent us from practicing the love and compassion that God calls us to demonstrate to those around us.

Relatable Examples of the Temptation to Prioritize Ourselves

The temptation to prioritize our own needs can be observed in many areas of life. Perhaps we experience it in our work life, when we are so focused on advancing our careers that we neglect the people around us — whether that means overlooking a colleague who needs support or failing to spend time with our families. In an attempt to climb the ladder, we may justify our actions by telling ourselves that "it's just temporary" or "I'm doing this for the future," but at what cost?

In relationships, it can manifest as the tendency to demand things from others that we're unwilling to offer ourselves. For example, if we're in a marriage, we may expect our spouse to meet all of our emotional needs without offering the same in return. We may demand time, attention, or affection without considering how the other person feels. Similarly, we might act selfishly with friends or family, withdrawing from their needs when they become inconvenient to us or when we're too preoccupied with our own struggles.

The temptation to put ourselves first can also appear in more subtle ways, such as when we choose comfort over service. When we encounter someone in need — whether it's a friend who needs a listening ear, a stranger who needs help, or a coworker who needs support — we might think, "I'm too busy right now" or "I don't have the emotional energy to get involved." We may justify our actions by thinking that taking care of ourselves is more important, when in reality, caring for others is what truly helps us grow in love, humility, and service.

The Spiritual Danger of Self-Centeredness

The spiritual danger of consistently putting our needs above others is that it fosters a self-centered mindset, which is diametrically opposed to the selfless love Jesus calls us to live out. Jesus Himself showed us the ultimate example of selflessness. In Philippians 2:5-8, Paul writes:

> "In your relationships with one another, have the same mindset as Christ Jesus: Who, being in very nature God, did not consider equality with God something to be used to his own advantage; rather, he made himself nothing by taking the very nature of a servant, being made in human likeness. And being found in appearance as a man, he humbled himself by becoming obedient to death—even death on a cross!"

Jesus, though fully God, did not seek His own comfort or elevate Himself over others. He chose to humble Himself, taking on the nature of a servant, even enduring suffering and death for the sake of others. This is the ultimate example of putting others before ourselves.

When we succumb to the temptation of putting our needs above others, we fail to live up to this example. Instead of showing the world the sacrificial love of Christ, we show a love that is self-serving, conditional, and limited. We miss the opportunity to demonstrate the grace and generosity that flows from a life surrendered to God's will.

The Dangers of Prioritizing Our Own Needs

1. **Strained Relationships:** *When we are consistently focused on ourselves, it can damage our relationships with others. Relationships thrive on mutual love and care, not on one-sidedness. If we are always taking and never giving, those around us will inevitably feel neglected, unimportant, or taken advantage of. This can create distance and tension in our friendships, families, and marriages.*

2. **Lack of Spiritual Growth:** *Putting others first is integral to spiritual maturity. Jesus taught that the greatest commandment is to love God with all our heart, soul, and mind, and the second is like it: to love our neighbor as ourselves (Matthew 22:37-39). The call to love others requires sacrifice, humility, and empathy. When we are preoccupied with our own needs, we miss out on the spiritual growth that comes from serving others. We stagnate in our faith because we fail to act as the hands and feet of Jesus.*

3. **Selfishness Breeds More Selfishness:** *The temptation to focus on our own needs becomes a cycle. The more we focus on ourselves, the more we are drawn to do so. Over time, it becomes harder to break free from this mindset, and we can become increasingly consumed by our own desires and comfort. We may feel like we're always entitled to something more — more rest, more recognition, more convenience — but this only leaves us discontent, and the endless pursuit of self-fulfillment never truly satisfies.*

4. **Loss of Compassion:** *When we are self-centered, we stop seeing the needs of others. Compassion arises from seeing others' struggles and seeking to alleviate them. But when our world revolves around our own comfort and needs, we are less likely to notice or respond to the hurts of others. In fact, we may even become irritated when someone else's need requires us to sacrifice something. Compassion requires vulnerability, humility, and the willingness to step outside of ourselves to meet the needs of others, and this is often at odds with our natural instinct to preserve our own comfort.*

Overcoming the Temptation to Put Ourselves First

So how can we resist the temptation to put our own needs above others? How can we cultivate a heart that reflects the selflessness of Christ? Here are a few thoughts:

1. **Remember the Example of Jesus:** *As we've already seen, Jesus is our model for selflessness. When we look to Him, we are reminded that true fulfillment comes not from self-indulgence but from serving others. Jesus washed His disciples' feet, fed the hungry, healed the sick, and ultimately laid down His life for the world. His life was marked by sacrificial love. By following His example, we can begin to shift our focus from our own desires to the needs of those around us.*

2. **Practice Humility:** *Humility is key to overcoming the temptation to prioritize ourselves. The apostle Paul encourages us to "do nothing out of selfish ambition or vain conceit, but rather, in humility value others above yourselves, not looking to your own interests but each of you to the interests of the others" (Philippians 2:3-4). Humility means recognizing that our needs are not more important than those of others, and that God has called us to serve rather than be served. It requires*

laying down our ego and putting the needs of others ahead of our own.

3. **Cultivate a Lifestyle of Service:** *When we choose to serve others, we train our hearts to live beyond ourselves. Serving doesn't always have to be grand or dramatic. It can be as simple as offering a listening ear, helping with household chores, or encouraging a friend who is struggling. Every act of service is a step toward breaking free from the self-centeredness that tempts us. When we choose to live for others, we reflect God's love more clearly.*

4. **Pray for a Heart of Compassion:** *Sometimes, the temptation to put ourselves first is rooted in a lack of empathy. When we're caught up in our own worries and struggles, it's hard to see the pain or need of others. But when we pray for a heart of compassion, asking God to open our eyes to the needs around us, we start to develop a genuine concern for others. Prayer is a powerful tool in changing our hearts and renewing our perspective.*

5. **Remember the Eternal Reward:** *Lastly, we must remember that God sees and rewards acts of service. Jesus reminds us in Matthew 25:40, "Whatever you did for one of the least of these brothers and sisters of mine, you did for me." When we serve others, we are ultimately serving Christ. And though we may not always receive recognition or thanks from others, God knows and will honor our sacrifices. Our reward is not in earthly accolades but in the eternal joy of living for His purposes.*

The temptation to put our own needs above others is one that we all face at various points in life. It's easy to justify selfishness and self-focus in a world that encourages individualism. However, as followers of Christ, we are called to a different standard — one that prioritizes the needs of others, just as Jesus put our needs before His own. Overcoming this temptation requires humility, compassion, and a willingness to serve, but it is also an opportunity for growth in our relationship with God and with others.

No matter how often we fall into the temptation of self-centeredness, we can take heart in the fact that God's grace is greater than our failures. He offers forgiveness and transformation, empowering us to live a life of love and service. Through His grace, we can learn to prioritize others, reflecting His selfless love and bringing glory to His name.

No One Is Beyond God's Grace

Finally, it is essential to remember that despite the reality of temptation and sin, no one is beyond God's grace. The depth of our struggles and the magnitude of our failures do not determine the extent of God's forgiveness. God's grace is limitless and is available to anyone who turns to Him in repentance. Sin, in all its forms, is not the final word over our lives. God's love and mercy are greater than our sin, and through Christ, we are offered redemption.

The Bible assures us that "Where sin increased, grace increased all the more" (Romans 5:20). There is no sin so great that it cannot be forgiven. No matter how many times we fail, God's grace is sufficient. Jesus' death on the cross paid the price for all sin, and His resurrection offers us the hope of new life.

When we struggle with temptation, we can take comfort in knowing that we are not alone. God's grace is always available to help us overcome our weaknesses. We are not defined by our failures but by the love of God that is poured out through Christ. No one is beyond His reach, and no sin is beyond His ability to forgive.

Temptation and sin are an inevitable part of the human experience, but the good news is that God's grace is greater still. Each of us faces the pull of temptation in various forms, whether through gossip, laziness, bitterness, pride, or indulgence. But God's grace offers forgiveness and transformation for anyone who seeks it. Through His strength, we can resist the temptation that tries to control us, and through His love, we are empowered to walk in obedience. No matter how far we fall, God is ready to extend His grace and draw us back to Himself.

Closing Prayer:

Jesus, Thanks for walking with us through the messy middle. For every tear, eye-roll, or awkward moment of "Wow, I really needed that," I'm grateful. Help the reader leave this chapter not with more shame, but with more hope. You're not done with them. Not even close. And You love them—even when they ugly cry. Amen.

Chapter 3: The Power of Grace and Forgiveness

Opening Prayer:

Lord, Let today be the day guilt gets evicted and grace moves in. Please pry the reader's fingers off the spiritual scorecard they keep tucked under their pillow. Remind them that You're not waiting for them to earn Your love—you already gave it. Help them experience grace like a warm blanket, not a lecture. And if they're skeptical, prove it. You're good at that. Amen.

"The Grace He'll Never Understand"

He never really got it.

Not the damage. Not the silence. Not the birthdays missed or the tears I couldn't soothe no matter how tightly I held our daughters, Kristen and Madison, in my arms.

He had a way of looking at the past like it was a distant film—grainy, out of focus, just moments that "didn't work out," as if walking away from your children was the equivalent of quitting a gym membership.

He'd always been charming. Confident. Surrounded by people who affirmed whatever version of the truth he was selling at the time. "You did what you had to do," they said. "That's just unreasonable."

But rights aren't the same as righteousness.

And moving on, for him, meant moving out of his children's lives— emotionally first, then physically across the country, then relationally—until there was nothing left but unanswered questions and two daughters who grew up thinking maybe they weren't worth being present for.

I carried the weight of it for years. I had to.

At first, I was furious. Not just at him, but at God. Because where was grace in this? Where was justice? Just because he and I got it wrong and failed, doesn't mean the girls should be alienated. They shouldn't be punished for my failure. How do you explain to your girls that the man who promised to be their protector just decided not to be?

The hardest part was that he didn't leave in a storm. No slammed doors or dramatic goodbyes. He just slowly faded. A few missed events. A canceled weekend visit. Then suddenly, a move across the country, a new woman. A new life. And his girls? An afterthought.

He'd call occasionally. Say vague things like, "I hope you girls are doing okay." Or, "You'll understand when you're older (yeah, they still do not understand and they are older)." He never asked about what he missed, what he broke in them. He mainly just spoke to them about his life, his events, his world, on the few occasions he decided to speak to them at all. On his terms. That didn't last long before the girls didn't want his terms and he didn't want the full picture, only the version that allowed him to sleep at night.

Once, years later, he came to visit with his new family. Kristen was in college by then, confident and gracious—everything I had prayed over her life. He acted like nothing had ever gone wrong. Asked about classes. Smiled too much. She said it was like watching a stranger perform in a play called Fatherhood. Madison was just indifferent at this point.

"I don't think he knows what he lost," she told me. "And I don't think he wants to."

And that stuck with me.

Because how do you forgive someone who doesn't ask for it? Who doesn't even seem to know they need it (I knew I needed his for the wrongs I committed)?

That was the question I carried into every Sunday sermon and quiet morning with my Bible. For a long time, I kept hoping for the moment—a grand apology for the girls, the "I see it now," the tears and the turning around. But it never came.

What came instead was grace.

Not loud or dramatic. Just soft. Slow.

I remember reading Romans 5:6 one morning: "While we were still weak, at the right time Christ died for the ungodly."

Not when we understood. Not when we repented. While we were still in the dark. Still justifying ourselves.

It hit me like a whisper from heaven: He may never know what he's done. But you do. And you still get to choose.

So I chose.

Not to excuse. Not to forget.

But to release.

I stopped waiting for closure from someone who didn't have the capacity to give it. I stopped rehearsing what I'd say if he ever "came to his senses." I stopped holding onto the bitterness that, frankly, was poisoning me far more than it was punishing him.

Instead, I started praying for him. Not because he deserved it, but because I needed it.

I asked God to show him grace—even if he never asked for it himself. I asked God to soften his heart, open his eyes, and—maybe hardest of all—to bless his life.

Because that's what grace is.

Unmerited.

Unfair.

Unearned.

And completely life-changing—for the giver, even when the receiver stays unchanged.

Forgiveness didn't rewrite history. It didn't fill the holes in our daughters' childhoods. But it did free me from living in reaction to a man who was still clinging to his justifications.

And over time, I saw grace do something even more beautiful: it multiplied in Kristen and Madison.

They set boundaries, yes. They protected their hearts. But they didn't grow up bitter. They didn't repeat the cycle. They became women who knew their worth and extended mercy to people who hadn't earned it— because they saw their mother do it first.

That's the real power of grace.

He may never understand what he walked away from. He may never sit with the weight of what it meant for Kristen to stop waiting for birthday calls, or for Madison to stop caring where he went. He may always believe the lie that he "did what he had to do."

But I know the truth.

And I know the God who met me in the ache, who reminded me that while I was still weak—while we were all still lost—He chose to love, to die, to forgive.

So I forgive him.

Not because he asked. Not because he deserves it.

But because grace has changed me.

And that's something he'll never take away.

Grace is one of the most profound and transformative concepts in the Christian faith. It is the unmerited favor of God, freely given to humanity despite our shortcomings and failures. The power of grace lies in its ability to completely change us from the inside out, providing healing, restoration, and a new way of living. In this chapter, we will explore the transformative power of God's grace, understand the biblical foundation for grace and forgiveness, and encourage readers to embrace forgiveness both from God and towards others.

1. The Transformative Gift of God's Grace

At its core, grace is God's unconditional love and favor given to us, not because of our works, but because of His love and mercy. In the New Testament, the Apostle Paul writes extensively about grace. In his letter to the Ephesians, Paul says:

"For it is by grace you have been saved, through faith—and this is not from yourselves, it is the gift of God—not by works, so that no one can boast." (Ephesians 2:8-9, NIV)

Here, Paul emphasizes that grace is not earned; it is a gift from God. It is through grace that we are saved, and salvation comes by faith. This grace is what transforms us; it changes our hearts, renews our minds, and empowers us to live a life pleasing to God. Grace is not just a one-time act but an ongoing work in the life of every believer.

The idea of transformation through grace is not just a theological concept; it is a lived reality for millions of Christians around the world. Grace does not leave us as we were before; it redefines our identity, purpose, and direction in life.

2. Grace as a Life-Changing Force

Grace is not passive; it is an active, dynamic force that leads to transformation. Consider the words of the Apostle Paul in his second letter to the Corinthians:

"Therefore, if anyone is in Christ, the new creation has come: The old has gone, the new is here!" (2 Corinthians 5:17, NIV)

This verse highlights the radical nature of the transformation that occurs when we encounter God's grace. We are not merely improved or refined versions of our old selves, but we are made new. Our past failures, sins, and mistakes no longer define us. The grace of God makes us new creations, with a new identity and purpose.

One of the most powerful examples of grace in the Bible is the story of Saul of Tarsus, later known as the Apostle Paul. Saul was a violent persecutor of Christians, consenting to the imprisonment and death of believers. However, God's grace broke into Saul's life in a profound way on the road to Damascus.

"As he neared Damascus on his journey, suddenly a light from heaven flashed around him. He fell to the ground and heard a voice say to him, 'Saul, Saul, why are you persecuting me?' 'Who are you, Lord?' Saul asked. 'I am Jesus, whom you are persecuting,' he replied." (Acts 9:3-5, NIV)

In that moment, Saul encountered the grace of God, and it transformed him completely. Saul's hatred and violence toward Christians were replaced by love and zeal for the gospel of Jesus Christ. Saul went from being a persecutor of Christians to one of the greatest advocates for the faith. This transformation is a powerful testament to the transformative nature of God's grace. No matter how deep our sin or how far we may have strayed, God's grace is more than sufficient to bring about a total transformation in our lives.

3. Biblical Stories of Grace in Action

There are many stories in the Bible that illustrate the transformative power of God's grace. Let us look at two more examples that emphasize the radical nature of grace.

The Prodigal Son (Luke 15:11-32)

The Parable of the Prodigal Son is a story told by Jesus that encapsulates the power of grace and forgiveness. In the story, a younger son demands his inheritance from his father and goes to a distant country, where he squanders all his wealth in reckless living. When a famine strikes, the son finds himself in dire need and decides to return to his father, hoping to be accepted back as a servant.

The turning point of the story comes when the father sees his son from a distance, and instead of rebuking him, he runs to embrace him. The father says:

"For this son of mine was dead and is alive again; he was lost and is found." (Luke 15:24, NIV)

This parable is a powerful illustration of God's grace. No matter how far we may have wandered, no matter how much we have sinned, God's grace is always ready to welcome us back. The father's actions show us that God's grace is not conditional on our worthiness but is freely given because of His love for us. The Prodigal Son is a beautiful reminder that God is always ready to forgive and restore those who turn back to Him, no matter their past mistakes.

The Woman Caught in Adultery (John 8:1-11)

Another powerful story of grace is the account of the woman caught in adultery. The religious leaders bring the woman to Jesus, accusing her of sin and demanding that she be stoned, as prescribed by the law. But Jesus responds with grace and wisdom:

"Let any one of you who is without sin be the first to throw a stone at her." (John 8:7, NIV)

One by one, the accusers leave, and Jesus remains with the woman. He says:

_"Woman, where are they? Has no one condemned you?"
_"No one, sir," she said.
"Then neither do I condemn you," Jesus declared. "Go now and leave your life of sin." (John 8:10-11, NIV)

This interaction is a powerful example of God's grace in action. Jesus does not condemn the woman for her sin but offers her forgiveness and the opportunity for transformation. Grace does not excuse sin but provides the opportunity for repentance and a new way of living. The woman's life is forever changed by the grace extended to her by Jesus, and she is given the chance to live differently, free from the condemnation of her past.

4. The Importance of Accepting Forgiveness

God desires to make it clear to us that we are forgiven, and He wants us to know for sure that we are free from the burden of guilt and shame. This assurance is vital for our spiritual growth and emotional well-being. In 1 John 1:9, the Apostle John assures us of God's forgiveness:

"If we confess our sins, he is faithful and just and will forgive us our sins and purify us from all unrighteousness." (1 John 1:9, NIV)

Confession is an important step in receiving God's forgiveness, but it is also essential that we accept that forgiveness and walk in the freedom it brings. Many believers struggle with guilt and shame even after they have confessed their sins to God. This is often because they do not fully accept the grace that has been offered to them.

One of the most powerful things we can do is to accept God's forgiveness and trust in His promises. When we embrace God's grace, we release ourselves from the weight of past mistakes and move forward in the freedom that Christ provides. We are no longer defined by our failures but by the love and grace of God.

5. The Vital Importance of Forgiving Others

While receiving God's forgiveness is crucial, the Bible also teaches that we must forgive others. Jesus spoke extensively about forgiveness, and He made it clear that forgiveness is not optional for Christians. In the Lord's Prayer, He instructs us to pray:

"Forgive us our debts, as we also have forgiven our debtors." (Matthew 6:12, NIV)

This is not merely a request; it is a command. Jesus goes on to explain the importance of forgiveness in Matthew 6:14-15:

"For if you forgive other people when they sin against you, your heavenly Father will also forgive you. But if you do not forgive others their sins, your Father will not forgive your sins." (Matthew 6:14-15, NIV)

Forgiveness is essential to our relationship with God. It is a reflection of the grace we have received and a necessary step in maintaining a healthy relationship with God. When we hold onto unforgiveness, we allow bitterness and resentment to take root in our hearts. This can hinder our spiritual growth and prevent us from experiencing the fullness of God's love and grace.

The Power of Forgiving Others: A Modern Example

A modern example of grace and forgiveness in action can be seen in the life of Corrie ten Boom, a Holocaust survivor who became a Christian author and speaker. During World War II, Corrie and her family were arrested for hiding Jews from the Nazis. After her imprisonment and the death of her sister, Betsie, in the concentration camps, Corrie struggled with unforgiveness toward the guards who had mistreated her.

After the war, Corrie was invited to speak in Germany about God's forgiveness. One day, after a speech in which she shared the message of forgiveness, one of the very guards who had been responsible for her suffering approached her. He extended his hand and asked for her forgiveness. In that moment, Corrie felt the deep conflict within her heart. But remembering the grace of God that had forgiven her, she chose to forgive him. She later wrote:

"And I prayed, 'Jesus, I cannot forgive him. Give me Your forgiveness.' As I took his hand, the most incredible thing happened. From my shoulder, along my arm, and through my hand, a current seemed to pass from me to him. While into my heart sprang a love for this stranger that almost overwhelmed me."

This act of forgiveness was a powerful demonstration of the transformative power of grace. Just as Corrie had been forgiven by God, she chose to extend that same grace to others. In doing so, she experienced the freedom and healing that comes from forgiveness.

6. Moving Forward in Grace

Forgiveness is not always easy, but it is essential for our emotional and spiritual health. Holding onto unforgiveness is like carrying a heavy burden that weighs us down and keeps us from moving forward in God's plan for our lives. When we choose to forgive, we release ourselves from that burden and make room for God's healing and peace.

God wants us to experience the full freedom of His grace. He wants us to know, without a doubt, that we are forgiven, and He desires that we extend that same forgiveness to others. When we embrace God's grace and forgive others, we open the door for God to work in and through us in ways that we could never imagine.

As you reflect on the power of grace and forgiveness, I encourage you to take a step of faith. If there are areas in your life where you are holding onto unforgiveness, bring those to God and ask Him for the strength to forgive. If you are struggling to accept God's forgiveness, remember that His grace is more than sufficient for you. You are loved, forgiven, and made new in Christ.

Let go of the past, embrace the forgiveness God offers, and move forward in the power of His grace.

Closing Prayer:

Father, Thank You for grace that doesn't keep receipts. Let this reader walk away from this chapter feeling lighter, freer, and maybe even smiling (or at least breathing deeper). Let them know that they are loved—even when they burn the spiritual casserole. Amen.

Part 2- Practical Steps to Grow Closer to Him

Chapter 4: Building a Relationship with God - Practical Steps to Grow Closer to Him

Opening Prayer:

Hey God, We're talking "relationship" now—not "religious routine," not "checklist," not "awkward small talk at a holy networking event." Help the reader drop the act and lean into the real. Teach them how to talk to You when they're annoyed, excited, tired, scared or stuck in traffic. Let this be where faith stops feeling like a job and starts feeling like home. Amen.

"When God Held Us Both"

At 23 weeks pregnant, I boarded a plane with a belly full of fear and a baby who was dying.

*Her name was already chosen—**Kristen**. We had picked it early, before we ever knew her tiny life would be defined by words I had to learn to pronounce just to understand what was happening. Congenital Cystic Adenomatoid Malformation. Non-immune fetal hydrops. Words that came with grim statistics and solemn doctors. Words that said: She won't survive unless we act—and even then...*

Even then.

I was terrified. Not the kind of fear you get before a job interview or a thunderstorm. This was primal, deep, silent fear—the kind you feel in your bones at 2 a.m. while pressing a hand against your stomach and whispering, Please, please just stay alive.

They told us she had fluid building around her tiny heart and lungs. That her left lung was malformed and growing like a balloon, crushing everything inside her. That her heart was barely functioning. That this was terminal. That unless we underwent open fetal surgery, she wouldn't make it.

So we flew across the country.

The day of the surgery, they put me under anesthesia. I remember praying as they wheeled me into the OR, God, I don't even know what to ask for anymore. Just be there. Just be in that room, and have YOUR way.

They opened my womb, pulled her partially from my body—this daughter I hadn't yet held—and removed her left lung. Then they placed her back inside me, stitched us both up, and told me the next few days would be critical.

I woke up groggy, hurting, confused—but still pregnant.

Still pregnant.

That was the first miracle.

The second was learning to breathe again when I couldn't.

Two days later, I stopped breathing. My lungs filled with fluid. My blood pressure tanked. I was rushed to the ICU where machines took over what my body couldn't do. I was barely conscious, aware only of nurses shouting and the cold fear gripping my chest tighter than any monitor ever could.

And in the middle of all that, I prayed—not eloquent, not theologically polished prayers. Just Help. Just God, please. Just don't let her lose me.

And He was there.

Not in flashing lights or parted skies. But in the steady hands of nurses. In the breath that returned. In the slow, inching return to stability.

And for weeks, I lay there. Waiting. Hoping. Still pregnant.

Kristen was born at 30 weeks, weighing just over three pounds, a single lung, and a spirit I can only describe as God-breathed. She needed machines. She needed help. But she was here.

Alive.

Fighting.

Our miracle.

The world saw wires and tubes. I saw grace.

Through it all, something else had been happening—not just inside my body, but inside my soul. A kind of slow rebuilding I hadn't expected. Because as much as Kristen was being saved physically, God was quietly saving me spiritually.

I had grown up believing in God, sure. But this... this wasn't religion. This was relationship. This was holding nothing back and letting Him in when I had absolutely nothing left.

I learned to pray differently. I stopped demanding. I started surrendering. I stopped saying, God, save her or I can't survive and started whispering, God, Your will is better than mine, even when I don't understand.

That surrender didn't come easily. Some days I clung to control like it was the only thing keeping me from falling apart. Other days I let go completely and just sat in silence, waiting. Listening.

That was something else I learned—how to listen.

Not just to Scripture, though that became my lifeline. But to the quiet nudges in my heart. The sudden peace that made no sense. The warmth in the room when I felt alone. The verse that popped up just when I needed it. I started praying more and more, talking to God like a friend. Some prayers were messy. Angry. Some were nothing but tears on the soaked pillow. And yet, every time, He met me there.

I didn't become perfect. I became honest. And in that honesty, I found comfort.

Psalm 34:18 became my anthem: "The Lord is close to the brokenhearted and saves those who are crushed in spirit." He was close. He was so close.

Kristen eventually came home. Tiny, resilient, mine. She grew. She thrived. She smiled with her whole face. And every breath she took reminded me: God is still in the miracle business.

But the bigger miracle, I think, was what He did in me.

He taught me that grace isn't always loud. That sometimes the greatest healing comes not from fixing our circumstances, but from changing our hearts.

I didn't just survive that season—I was transformed by it.

I learned to trust. To surrender. To speak, yes—but also to be silent. To fear—but not be ruled by it. To hope, not in outcomes, but in Him.

Kristen's story will always be marked by scars and survival.

Mine will be marked by grace.

Building a deeper relationship with God is one of the most profound and transformative experiences a person can have. Prayer, communication with God, and finding His presence in everyday life are all critical aspects of this spiritual journey. In this chapter, we will explore how to pray authentically, step away from overly formalized approaches, and embrace a more personal, conversational connection with God. Additionally, we will look at how we can see God's presence in the world around us, in the smallest acts of kindness and the beauty of nature. Through these practices, we can deepen our relationship with God, listening for His voice, receiving His answers, and finding Him in every corner of our daily lives.

1: Praying Authentically, Not Formally

1.1 The Nature of Prayer

Prayer is often viewed as a ritual or a set of words recited in a particular way, but at its core, prayer is about relationship. It is the vehicle through which we communicate with God, express our hearts, and listen to His voice. When we pray authentically, we move beyond mere formality and enter into a conversation with God. This is not to say that formal prayers or set prayers don't have value, but rather that prayer should be something that feels real, personal, and genuine to us.

Think of prayer as a conversation with a trusted friend or family member. When we speak to them, we do not use overly formal language or follow rigid rules. Instead, we speak naturally, sharing our joys, frustrations, fears, and hopes. In the same way, we can talk to God as we would to someone who loves us deeply and intimately.

1.2 Acknowledge God's Presence

The first step toward authentic prayer is simply acknowledging God's presence. Take a moment to recognize that He is here, right now, and that He desires to hear from you. This acknowledgment can be done in silence, in a short prayer of gratitude, or even in a mental acknowledgment as you go about your day.

For example, if you're walking outside, take a deep breath and say, "Lord, thank You for this beautiful world. I know You are with me right now." This can serve as an opening to deeper conversation.

1.3 Speak from the Heart

Many people struggle with what to say in prayer because they feel the need to follow a formula. The beauty of authentic prayer is that you do not have to have a perfect script. Speak from your heart. Share your feelings, your worries, your gratitude, your struggles. God knows what is in your heart, so there is no need for pretense.

Consider a situation from modern life. Imagine you've had a tough day at work and you're feeling overwhelmed. Instead of trying to articulate a perfect prayer, simply tell God what you're feeling: "God, I'm really struggling today. I feel drained and frustrated, and I need Your help. Please give me peace and strength." You might not have the right words, but your honesty and vulnerability are what matter most.

1.4 Use Scriptures to Guide Your Prayers

If you are unsure of how to pray or need help finding words, turn to Scripture. The Bible is filled with prayers and expressions of deep emotion that can resonate with us in our own lives. Psalms are particularly helpful for expressing sorrow, joy, thanksgiving, or longing, and can be used as a springboard for your own prayer.

For instance, Psalm 42:1-2 says, "As the deer pants for streams of water, so my soul pants for you, my God. My soul thirsts for God, for the living God. When can I go and meet with God?" These words can express a longing for God's presence in a way that we may feel in our own hearts.

Take the time to personalize such verses. If you're feeling distant from God, pray something like: "Lord, my soul longs for You like the deer longs for water. I feel distant, but I know You are near. Draw me close to You today."

1.5 Be Honest and Open

Authentic prayer is marked by honesty. God knows our hearts, and there's no need to hide from Him. If you are angry, frustrated, or confused, share that with God. He is a safe place for your honest feelings.

Consider the example of David in the Psalms. He was often honest with God about his fears, struggles, and emotions. In Psalm 13, David cries out, "How long, O Lord? Will you forget me forever? How long will you hide your face from me?" This raw honesty allowed David to process his emotions while still maintaining his faith.

1.6 Be Silent and Listen

While speaking to God is essential, listening is just as important. Prayer is a two-way conversation. It's easy to focus on what we need to say, but God also wants to speak to us. In your prayer time, allow space for silence. God's voice may come through a thought, a feeling, or a gentle prompting in your spirit.

Jesus often withdrew to quiet places to pray and listen to God. Luke 5:16 tells us, "But Jesus often withdrew to lonely places and prayed." Silence and stillness are vital for hearing God's voice.

2: Journaling and Speaking to God in Daily Life

2.1 Journaling as a Conversation with God

Journaling can be an incredibly effective way to speak to God and track your spiritual growth. Writing down your prayers can help you process your thoughts, articulate your feelings, and reflect on God's work in your life.

To begin journaling, set aside a specific time each day to write. It can be as simple as starting with a prayer: "Lord, today I am grateful for Your love, and I want to listen for Your voice as I write." Write your thoughts, ask questions, or pour out your struggles. When you look back over your journal, you may see how God has answered prayers, comforted you, or led you in unexpected ways.

In addition, journaling allows you to keep track of what you feel God is saying to you, helping you discern His will over time. For example, if you are praying about a decision in your life, write down your thoughts and reflect on them regularly. God may give you clarity through this process.

2.2 Speaking to God Throughout the Day

Prayer is not limited to a specific time of day or a particular posture. We can speak to God in the middle of our daily activities. Whether you're driving, working, or spending time with family, God is always available to listen.

Imagine you are in a meeting at work and feeling anxious about an upcoming presentation. In that moment, you can silently pray, "Lord, help me stay calm and trust You. Please give me wisdom and the words to speak." This is an example of spontaneous prayer, where you can bring God into the details of your life.

Similarly, if you're interacting with others and feel frustration building up, ask God for patience: "God, please help me to be patient and loving in this situation. Let Your peace reign in my heart."

2.3 Practicing Presence and Awareness

One way to speak to God in daily life is by practicing presence and awareness. This means paying attention to the small, mundane moments that often go unnoticed and acknowledging God's presence in those moments.

For example, when you sit down for a meal, instead of rushing through it, take a moment to thank God for the food and the hands that prepared it. As you look out the window and see the beauty of the sky, you can whisper a prayer of gratitude: "Thank You, Lord, for the beauty of this day. Your creation is amazing."

The more you practice this awareness, the more you will find yourself connecting with God throughout your day, no matter what you're doing.

3: Seeing God in the Everyday

3.1 Finding God in Nature

Nature is one of the clearest places where we can see the fingerprints of God. From the vastness of the ocean to the intricate beauty of a flower, the natural world is filled with evidence of God's creativity and power.

Psalm 19:1 declares, "The heavens declare the glory of God; the skies proclaim the work of his hands." When you are out in nature, take time to notice the details—the colors, the smells, the sounds. These are reminders that God is all around us.

When you go for a walk in the park or stand in awe of a sunset, take a moment to thank God for His creation. You can pray something like, "Lord, thank You for the beauty of the world You've made. Help me to see Your hand in everything around me."

3.2 Recognizing God's Presence in Acts of Kindness

Another way to see God in everyday life is through acts of kindness. God's love is evident in the way people care for one another, show compassion, and help those in need. Every act of love is a reflection of God's heart.

If you receive kindness from someone, take a moment to recognize it as a gift from God. Perhaps someone holds the door for you when your hands are full, or a friend checks in on you when you're feeling down. In those moments, you can pray, "Thank You, Lord, for this person's kindness. It is a reminder of Your love and care for me."

Also, look for opportunities to extend kindness to others. In doing so, you become a vessel for God's love and grace. A simple act, like helping a neighbor or offering a word of encouragement, can be a reflection of God's work in your life.

3.3 Seeing God in Everyday Conversations

God often speaks to us through the people around us. A conversation with a friend, a family member, or even a stranger may contain the very words you need to hear. As you engage with others, stay attuned to God's presence.

For instance, someone might share an encouraging word that resonates with you, or you may have a deep, meaningful conversation that leads to new insights. In these moments, recognize that God may be speaking to you through the people He has placed in your life.

Building a deeper relationship with God requires intentional effort, but the rewards are immeasurable. Through authentic prayer, journaling, and speaking to God throughout the day, we open ourselves to deeper communication with Him. We also begin to see God's presence in the everyday moments of life—in nature, in acts of kindness, and in the conversations we have with others. By practicing presence and cultivating an awareness of God's love, we draw closer to Him and invite His guidance, wisdom, and peace into every area of our lives.

As you move forward in your relationship with God, remember that it is not about perfection but about authenticity. God desires your heart, and as you give it to Him, you will experience a deeper connection with the One who loves you beyond measure.

Closing Prayer:

Thank You, Lord, For making Yourself available—even when we show up distracted, paralyzed by fear, or wearing spiritual pajamas. Bless this reader with a growing, real, heart-level friendship with You. Help them text You spiritually (or literally—we won't judge). Amen.

Chapter 5: Finding Balance in Faith and Fun

Opening Prayer:

God, You invented joy, so surely You're okay with us laughing in this chapter. Remind the reader that they don't have to be boring to be holy. Let this chapter break legalism, lighten spirits, and bring a holy chuckle or two. Help them see that fun isn't the enemy of faith—it might be the missing ingredient. Amen.

"The Joy of Lost Keys and Holy Interruptions"

It was Monday morning. The kind of Monday that starts with good intentions and ends with you talking to God through clenched teeth.

I had set my alarm early to get a jumpstart on the day—devotions, a brisk walk, maybe even a few minutes to sit in silence before the world exploded. I had plans. I had peace. And then, I couldn't find my keys.

I don't mean "misplaced." I mean lost. Like, vanished-into-thin-air-are-they-in-the-freezer-again lost.

I turned the house upside down. Couch cushions. Laundry basket. Dog bed. Nothing. I even checked my shoes, because hey, it's Monday, and anything's possible.

I muttered a desperate prayer: "Lord, You know where they are. Reveal them to me. Speak, for Your servant is late."

My walk was canceled. My devotional time was replaced with a frantic scavenger hunt. And by the time I finally found the keys—in my coat pocket, of course (a place I didn't look because we don't use coats everyday in Florida)—I was sweaty, five minutes behind schedule, and about 90% sure I needed a do-over on this whole "faith and joy" thing.

I worked at the U.S. Attorney's Office, which was about a 35 minute drive to work. Driving to work, I tried to reset. "It's fine," I told myself. "A Christian walks by faith, not by smooth mornings."

Then I hit traffic.

A big blinking sign announced, LEFT LANE CLOSED – MERGE RIGHT about three seconds too late, and I ended up stuck behind a truck carrying what I assume was a year's supply of gravel for the state of Alaska.

I may or may not have prayed for fire from heaven.

Instead, I got a sermon in my heart: "Patience produces perseverance." "Okay, God, but what if I don't want to persevere right now?"

That's the thing about walking in faith. Sometimes it looks like courage and confidence. Other times it looks like gritting your teeth behind a gravel truck while trying not to say things you'll have to repent for later.

Still, I made it to work.

I had barely walked through the door when my coworker, Tiffany, waved me over. She's sweet. She means well. But she also tells very long stories about her cat, her dreams, and occasionally both.

"All I wanted was to get to my emails before court," I told the Lord in my spirit.

But I stopped. I smiled. I listened.

It turned out Tiffany's mom had a health scare over the weekend. She was scared. I mean, really scared. And after about ten minutes, she looked at me and said, "I don't know why I'm telling you all this—I just feel like you actually care."

And there it was. A holy interruption. The kind that sneaks into your schedule wearing ordinary clothes and asks, Will you walk by faith, even now?

So I prayed with her. In the break room. Next to a microwave that was loudly reheating someone's questionable leftovers at 7:52 AM. Who eats leftovers at 7:52 AM? It wasn't dramatic or fancy. Just a quiet, simple prayer.

And when I finished, Tiffany wiped a tear and said, "That helped. Thank you."

She walked away, and I just stood there. No halo. No heavens opening. Just me, my morning caffeine, and this deep, steady joy in my chest.

Because in that moment, I knew: This is what it looks like to walk in faith and still embrace the joy of life.

It's not a glamorous journey. It's not uninterrupted. It's keys in your coat pocket and detours you didn't expect. It's coworkers in need and microwave prayers and a God who weaves glory into the mundane.

Joy doesn't mean everything goes right. It means you find God in the things that go wrong.

Later that day, I bumped into my neighbor on the way inside. She was newer, a little reserved. We exchanged the usual small talk—weather, mail, dogs—and then, out of nowhere, she asked, "You always seem so calm. Are you, like, religious or something?"

I laughed.

Because I had yelled at my houseplants that morning (don't worry, they were already dead. They didn't hear me). I had almost wept behind the gravel truck. I had definitely not felt calm.

But I told her, "I have faith. And I'm learning how to walk in it."

She nodded slowly. "I've been thinking about trying church again."

I smiled. "I'd be happy to go with you."

And just like that, another holy interruption.

Here's the truth: walking in faith doesn't always feel spiritual. Sometimes it feels like missing keys, spilled gravel, and last-minute prayers in break rooms.

But when you let go of the pressure to feel holy and just live with your heart open to God's presence, you start to notice something:

The joy was there all along.

In the detours.

In the interruptions.

In the small, ordinary moments where grace shows up quietly and whispers, Keep going. I'm with you.

And sometimes, that's all you need to smile—even behind a gravel truck.

There's a pervasive misconception in today's world that living a life of faith requires sacrificing fun and joy. Many people assume that to be faithful, one must retreat from worldly pleasures, avoid social gatherings, and relinquish moments of enjoyment for the sake of a more solemn, austere existence. However, this view is not only inaccurate, it's also limiting. A life of faith, when understood correctly, can be full of joy, laughter, and fulfillment. Faith doesn't mean removing yourself from the pleasures of life; rather, it means engaging in life in a way that aligns with your values, brings you peace, and allows you to grow spiritually.

In this chapter, we'll explore how you can walk in faith while still embracing the joy of life. We'll break down the misconception that faith and fun are mutually exclusive, share examples of wholesome, God-honoring ways to enjoy life that also appeal to nonbelievers, and provide tips for making mindful choices that allow you to fully enjoy life without compromising your values.

The Misconception of Faith and Sacrifice

For many, the idea of faith seems synonymous with denial—denial of personal pleasure, freedom, and enjoyment. In some religious circles, there's a belief that faith demands a life of solemnity and self-denial, as though true devotion requires sacrificing happiness or worldly experiences. However, this viewpoint doesn't accurately reflect the holistic nature of faith.

The Bible teaches that God delights in His creation and that life is a gift to be enjoyed in His presence. Psalm 16:11 says, "You make known to me the path of life; you will fill me with joy in your presence, with eternal pleasures at your right hand." This suggests that joy is not something we have to forfeit in our pursuit of a relationship with God but rather a gift that comes from being aligned with His will.

There's a reason why Christ came to earth—not just to offer salvation but to provide a model of life in abundance. In John 10:10, Jesus says, "I have come that they may have life, and have it to the full." Fullness of life doesn't mean a life devoid of enjoyment, but one that is rich in purpose, meaning, and genuine connection to others. Faith, when embraced rightly, can bring depth and fulfillment to our enjoyment of the world around us.

Faith and Fun Aren't Mutually Exclusive

The real challenge, then, lies in navigating a culture that often equates fun with excess or self-indulgence. How can we enjoy life without compromising our spiritual values? How do we reconcile faith with a desire for fun and social connection?

First and foremost, we must reframe our understanding of "fun" itself. Fun doesn't have to involve reckless behavior, excess, or activities that lead to negative consequences. Instead, fun can be found in moments of fellowship, creativity, adventure, and even rest—activities that can nurture both body and soul. The key is moderation, mindfulness, and intentionality.

Here are a few ways that faith and fun can go hand in hand:

1. **Socializing with Purpose**
   Social gatherings don't need to revolve around drinking or other unhealthy behaviors. Faith can lead to socializing with purpose—inviting friends over for game nights, potlucks, or movie marathons that promote healthy conversation and build stronger relationships. Being intentional about your time with others is a way of honoring God's design for community while enjoying life together.

2. **Outdoor Activities and Adventure**
   Taking part in outdoor activities is a wonderful way to enjoy God's creation. Hiking, camping, biking, and exploring new places can be spiritually refreshing and physically invigorating. These activities also offer opportunities for quiet reflection and connection with God, especially in the stillness of nature. Furthermore, enjoying nature can serve as a reminder of God's provision and beauty.

3. **Celebrations of Life**
   Parties, birthdays, weddings, and holidays can all be joyful occasions when centered around gratitude and love. Celebrating milestones with friends and family is an opportunity to share God's love and to recognize His blessings. These celebrations need not be over-the-top or extravagant; the simple joy of being together is enough to honor God and enjoy His creation.

4. **Art, Music, and Creativity**
   God is a creator, and as His image-bearers, we too have the capacity for creativity. Whether it's painting, writing, dancing, or playing music, the act of creation can be deeply fulfilling and spiritually enriching. Many forms of art can also serve as a form of worship, allowing you to connect with others while embracing your unique talents.

5. **Service and Volunteering**
   A truly fulfilling life is one that serves others. Faith can be

lived out through service to the community, whether by volunteering at a local shelter, mentoring youth, or contributing to charity. These activities are not only meaningful but often come with the bonus of creating lasting bonds and a sense of purpose.

Wholesome, God-Honoring Ways to Enjoy Life

Now let's explore a few examples of specific activities and practices that allow you to embrace life while honoring God, even in a world that may not share your faith. These are activities that appeal to both believers and nonbelievers and can be enjoyed with a joyful heart, knowing that they contribute to the flourishing of life.

1. **Community Meals and Gatherings**
   Gathering around a table with friends and family is a timeless way to enjoy life. It's a practice that transcends religious boundaries, and yet it can be deeply spiritual for believers. Sharing a meal provides an opportunity for connection, gratitude, and joy. The simple act of breaking bread together can deepen relationships, foster meaningful conversations, and create cherished memories. Jesus Himself frequently gathered with others over meals, and this practice remains a beautiful and accessible way to live out faith in a communal setting.

2. **Sports and Physical Activities**
   Engaging in sports or exercise is a great way to care for the body, build camaraderie, and relieve stress. Whether it's a friendly game of soccer, a tennis match, or just a run with friends, these activities can offer opportunities for enjoyment, growth, and social bonding. The Bible reminds us that our bodies are temples of the Holy Spirit (1 Corinthians 6:19), and taking care of our physical health can be an act of honoring God. Physical activities can also provide opportunities for

fellowship and collaboration with others who share a similar passion.

3. **Cultural Experiences**

   Exploring new cultures, whether through travel or local events, is an enriching experience that opens us up to the beauty and diversity of God's creation. Museums, theater performances, art exhibitions, and concerts can offer exposure to different perspectives and a greater appreciation for the creativity of others. These activities invite reflection and dialogue and can be opportunities to celebrate the richness of life that transcends religious or cultural boundaries.

4. **Mindfulness and Reflection**

   Taking time for quiet reflection, whether through journaling, meditation, or prayer, is an important aspect of nurturing your faith while staying grounded in the present moment. You can incorporate mindfulness practices that focus on gratitude and connection to God, which can help you embrace life fully without becoming overwhelmed by its demands. Being present in the moment allows you to experience the joy that comes from God's blessings without being distracted by the pressures of life.

Tips for Making Mindful Choices

Here are some practical tips for embracing life while staying true to your faith:

1. **Evaluate the Intent Behind Your Activities**

   Before engaging in any activity, take a moment to evaluate your intentions. Are you seeking to glorify God through this experience? Are you building relationships and contributing positively to the community? If your intent aligns with your values, then you can enjoy the activity with a clear conscience.

2. **Moderation is Key**

   You don't have to reject the world's pleasures outright, but it's essential to practice moderation. Whether it's indulging in food, entertainment, or other forms of enjoyment, balance is key. The Bible encourages self-control, and this can be a helpful guide when determining how much is too much.

3. **Create Boundaries that Protect Your Heart**
   It's important to set boundaries that align with your beliefs. If certain activities or environments tend to lead you away from God or tempt you into unhealthy behaviors, it's okay to step back or avoid them. Having boundaries allows you to engage in life fully while still maintaining your integrity.

4. **Surround Yourself with Positive Influences**
   Surrounding yourself with people who share your values will help you make wise choices. When you spend time with individuals who encourage you to grow spiritually and emotionally, you'll find that faith and fun coexist more naturally.

5. **Remember That True Joy Comes from God**
   Ultimately, true joy is a gift from God. While external circumstances and activities can bring temporary pleasure, lasting joy comes from being rooted in Christ. Remember to cultivate an attitude of gratitude and stay connected to the Source of all joy, allowing His presence to fill your life.

Faith and fun are not at odds; they complement each other beautifully when approached with intentionality and mindfulness. Living a life of faith does not require you to forfeit joy or retreat from the pleasures of the world. Instead, it calls you to engage with life in a way that honors God, builds community, and brings fulfillment. By making mindful choices, embracing the goodness of life, and sharing experiences with others, you can walk with joy, share in the abundance of life, and reflect God's love in all that you do.

So, go ahead—celebrate life with purpose, enjoy time with friends, explore new activities, and embrace the gift of laughter and joy. As you do so, you'll find that balance between faith and fun not only leads to personal growth but also brings glory to God.

Closing Prayer:

Jesus, Thanks for being the kind of Savior who went to weddings, told jokes, and probably would've loved a good meme. Help the reader not take themselves too seriously. Fill their life with joy, deep laughter, and You. Amen.

Chapter 6: Daily Habits for Spiritual Growth

Opening Prayer:

Lord, We're about to talk habits. Please don't let the reader run screaming. Replace the shame of past failed "quiet time plans" with excitement for small, doable steps. Help them realize it's not about perfection—it's about presence. And maybe keep their highlighters from drying out this time. Amen.

"Sanctified in the Grocery Store Aisle"

I used to think spiritual growth required something dramatic—maybe a weeklong retreat in the mountains, fasting on a mountaintop like Moses, or giving up carbs and social media at the same time (which, let's be honest, might be even harder than the mountaintop thing).

Turns out, sometimes God chooses to grow you right in the middle of aisle seven at the grocery store.

Let me explain.

It all started with a New Year's resolution. I told myself, This is the year I will grow spiritually. I even made a list. (Because what's more holy than color-coded intentions?) The list included things like "Read the Bible in a year," "Wake up at 5:30 a.m. for quiet time," and "Memorize the book of James."

You know where this is going, right?

By January 5th, I had read Genesis 1, hit snooze seven times, and accidentally memorized the ingredients to Pop-Tarts instead of James. I was already behind on my holy goals and starting to feel like maybe spiritual growth was only for monks and Instagram influencers with aesthetic prayer journals.

But then something weird started happening.

It began with a Post-it note.

I had scribbled "Be still and know" (Psalm 46:10) on it during a Sunday sermon and stuck it to my bathroom mirror. Honestly, I was aiming for spiritual ambiance, but mostly it ended up just stuck behind my deodorant.

Then one morning—while brushing my teeth and mentally rehearsing everything I needed to do before 7:00 a.m.—my eyes landed on that tiny note. "Be still and know."

And for two whole seconds, I stopped scrubbing my molars like a maniac. I stood still.

It wasn't dramatic. The heavens didn't open. But I breathed. And I realized, Oh. Maybe this is how it starts.

So I started adding little things. Not monk-level things—real things.

I played worship music in the car instead of historical fiction audiobooks. I prayed for coworkers while I stood in line at Whataburger (especially the one who constantly reheats fish in the office microwave). I started thanking God for random things—parking spots, clean socks, and that one pen that never runs out of ink.

And then came the grocery store incident.

I was in a hurry. (Aren't we always?) I had exactly 20 minutes to grab dinner, pick up allergy meds, and make it home before my sanity expired.

That's when I ran into her.

You know the type.

Long-winded. Slow-moving. Loves to chat in public like we're catching up after a ten-year separation even though we literally saw each other last Wednesday at church.

She cornered me somewhere between the canned corn and the gluten-free pancake mix.

"Oh hey, you!" she said, eyes lighting up. "I've been meaning to tell you about my nephew's cousin's dog's skin condition."

Lord, help me.

I smiled, nodded, and practiced the sacred art of active listening while glancing discreetly at my watch. But then she said something that stopped me cold.

"I've just felt so distant from God lately," she whispered. "Like I don't know how to find Him in all the noise."

Boom. Just like that, aisle seven became holy ground.

I put down my basket. I looked her in the eyes. And I told her what I'd been learning: that God isn't waiting for us to clear our calendars and chant by candlelight. He's in the seconds. The small things. The moments in between.

"I've started finding Him in the car, in the laundry pile, even in the grocery store," I said.

She blinked. "Really?"

I nodded. "Especially in the grocery store."

We laughed. Right there. Like weirdos near the shelf-stable taco shells. But it felt good.

It felt holy.

Because here's the truth: spiritual growth isn't always about doing more. Sometimes it's about noticing more. Being present. Making a habit of turning your thoughts toward God—ten seconds at a time.

After that day, I stopped obsessing over long prayer times and started aiming for frequent little prayers. I talked to God while doing laundry. I thanked Him while sweeping the floors. I sang worship songs while matching mismatched socks (which felt like a miracle in itself).

And you know what? I grew.

Not in a flashy, social-media-worthy kind of way. But in a quiet, steady, heart-deep way.

One day, a friend asked me, "What's changed? You seem… lighter."

I laughed and said, "Well, I gave up trying to perform spiritual growth and started just living with God."

She looked confused, so I added, "I realized it's not about grand gestures. It's about tiny habits that shift your heart."

Like pausing at a red light and saying, "Thank You, Lord."
Like praying for your boss before that awkward meeting.
Like whispering "Be still" while standing in a checkout line behind someone writing a check in 2025.

It all counts.

God isn't grading us on Bible chapters read or minutes spent praying with our eyes closed. He's just waiting for us to notice Him—in the morning routine, the workday stress, the everyday ordinary.

So if your life feels too busy for spiritual growth—good news.

You're in the perfect place for it.

You don't need a silent retreat.

You don't need a color-coded faith planner (though they are quite pretty).

You just need a willing heart, five spare minutes, and maybe a sticky note with a Bible verse tucked behind your deodorant.

Because God? He meets us there too.

In a world that moves at an increasingly fast pace, it can be difficult to prioritize spiritual growth amidst the many demands of daily life. The good news is that spiritual growth doesn't require monumental changes or overwhelming commitments. In fact, it can be cultivated in small but powerful ways that fit seamlessly into your day-to-day routines. Through simple, intentional habits, you can deepen your connection to God, strengthen your faith, and live with purpose and peace in the midst of your busy life.

This chapter will explore a variety of small but impactful habits that can help nurture your spiritual growth. From reading a verse a day to practicing gratitude, integrating worship music into your routine, and learning how to weave faith into the fabric of your everyday life, these habits will serve as the foundation for consistent spiritual development. With patience, commitment, and mindfulness, you can build a spiritual life that is both meaningful and sustainable.

Habit 1: Reading a Verse a Day

One of the most fundamental habits for spiritual growth is engaging with the Word of God regularly. The Bible is God's living and active word, and reading it daily can provide you with wisdom, encouragement, and guidance. While some might find it daunting to read long passages of scripture every day, starting with just one verse can have an incredibly powerful impact on your faith journey.

Why Reading a Verse a Day Matters

A single verse, when meditated upon, can speak volumes to your heart. The Bible tells us that God's word is a lamp to our feet and a light to our path (Psalm 119:105), which means that it has the power to illuminate our lives and help us navigate even the most challenging circumstances. Even on days when you don't have time for a long reading session, taking a moment to reflect on one verse can set the tone for your day and encourage your heart.

How to Get Started

To begin this habit, choose a time during the day when you can consistently read your verse. Some people prefer to read in the morning as a way to center themselves for the day ahead, while others may find it helpful to reflect on a verse in the evening to close their day. Regardless of when you choose, the key is consistency.

You can pick a verse at random, use a devotional or scripture app, or follow a Bible reading plan. Many Bible apps offer daily verse notifications, making it easy to engage with scripture even if you're short on time.

Deepening Your Understanding

As you read your verse, take a few moments to meditate on its meaning. What is God trying to speak to you through this scripture? How does it apply to your current life circumstances? Prayerfully reflect on the verse, allowing the Holy Spirit to guide you in understanding and applying it.

You can also journal your thoughts about the verse, writing down how it resonates with you or how it challenges you. Over time, this habit will deepen your knowledge of scripture and foster a more intimate relationship with God.

Habit 2: Practicing Gratitude

Gratitude is a powerful tool for spiritual growth. The act of giving thanks not only shifts our focus toward the blessings in our lives but also aligns our hearts with God's goodness. In 1 Thessalonians 5:16-18, Paul encourages believers to "rejoice always, pray without ceasing, give thanks in all circumstances; for this is the will of God in Christ Jesus for you." Gratitude is not merely an emotional response to good circumstances; it's a spiritual discipline that can transform our hearts and minds.

Why Gratitude Matters

When we practice gratitude, we acknowledge that all good things come from God (James 1:17). Gratitude helps us recognize His provision, even in the midst of hardship, and cultivates an attitude of humility and trust. It also reminds us of God's faithfulness, encouraging us to lean into His promises.

Regularly practicing gratitude can reduce stress, increase feelings of joy and contentment, and help us maintain a positive outlook on life. It shifts our focus from what we lack to what we have, fostering a spirit of abundance rather than scarcity.

How to Get Started

To cultivate gratitude, try setting aside a few minutes each day to write down things you are thankful for. You can do this in a dedicated journal or on a note app on your phone. This simple practice helps reframe your perspective and opens your eyes to the everyday blessings you may otherwise overlook.

Start with a list of three things you're grateful for each day. As you write, take time to reflect on why you're thankful for these things. Maybe it's the support of a friend, the beauty of a sunset, or the provision of your daily needs. Thank God specifically for each blessing and recognize His hand in all things.

Another way to practice gratitude is through prayer. As part of your daily prayer time, take a moment to offer thanks for both the big and small things in your life. This can be done before you ask God for anything, as a way to acknowledge His goodness and reignite your sense of awe.

Deepening Your Practice of Gratitude

You can make gratitude even more meaningful by practicing it in the face of challenges. When you encounter difficulty or disappointment, try to identify aspects of the situation for which you can be thankful. It may be hard at first, but as you intentionally look for the good, your heart will begin to shift, and you'll find more reasons to be grateful, even in the tough moments.

Habit 3: Listening to Worship Music or Podcasts

Another habit that can deeply impact your spiritual growth is incorporating worship music or podcasts into your daily routine. Worship music invites us into the presence of God and helps us focus our hearts on Him. Podcasts, particularly those that share biblical teaching, offer opportunities for learning and growth, even while on the go.

Why Worship Music and Podcasts Matter

Worship music serves as a powerful tool for spiritual connection. It helps us fix our eyes on God, praise Him for His goodness, and strengthen our faith. Psalm 95:1-2 says, "Come, let us sing for joy to the Lord; let us shout aloud to the Rock of our salvation." Singing and listening to worship can uplift our spirits, refresh our souls, and deepen our relationship with God.

Podcasts, on the other hand, offer a convenient way to receive biblical teaching and practical wisdom. Whether you're driving, exercising, or doing chores around the house, listening to a podcast can turn mundane tasks into opportunities for spiritual enrichment.

How to Get Started

You don't have to be a musician to engage in worship music. Simply choose songs that focus on God's attributes, such as His love, faithfulness, and sovereignty. You can listen to worship playlists on music streaming services or explore Christian radio stations. Try to make worship a part of your daily routine, whether it's in the morning to start your day or during moments of stress to recalibrate your heart.

For podcasts, look for ones that align with your spiritual goals. There are podcasts for every area of life—Bible teaching, prayer, marriage, parenting, and more. Some popular Christian podcasts offer deep dives into scripture, while others focus on practical applications of faith in everyday life. Experiment with different shows to find those that resonate with you.

Deepening Your Experience

While listening to worship music or podcasts, make it a point to reflect on what you're hearing. In worship, don't just let the music wash over you—actively engage your heart and mind. Sing along, if possible, and use the time to pray or meditate on the lyrics.

With podcasts, take notes on key takeaways or thoughts that resonate with you. Consider how the insights shared can be applied to your life, and be open to the ways God might be using these teachings to challenge you or deepen your faith.

Habit 4: Tips for Integrating Faith into a Busy Life

Many of us have hectic schedules and often feel like we're juggling a thousand different responsibilities. Yet, even in the midst of busyness, we can find ways to integrate our faith into our daily lives. The goal is not to compartmentalize your spiritual life but to weave faith into the fabric of your everyday routine.

Why Integration Matters

Integrating faith into your daily life means that your relationship with God is not confined to a set time or place. It becomes an ongoing, organic part of your life, influencing the way you think, speak, and act. It also allows you to experience God's presence throughout your day, not just during designated times of prayer or church services.

Colossians 3:17 encourages us to "do everything in the name of the Lord Jesus, giving thanks to God the Father through him." This means that whether you're working, spending time with family, or relaxing, you can do it all with a heart that seeks to honor God.

How to Get Started

1. **Turn Routine Tasks into Opportunities for Prayer**
   Whether you're cooking, commuting, or doing household chores, use these moments to pray. You can pray for guidance, thanksgiving, or simply connect with God in the midst of your

work. These small moments of prayer can help you stay grounded in God's presence throughout your day.

2. **Practice Mindful Reflection**

   During the course of your day, take short pauses to reflect on God's goodness. Whether you're sitting at your desk or waiting in line, take a moment to acknowledge His presence and offer thanks. This practice can keep your mind focused on Him amid the distractions of life.

3. **Serve Others**

   You can integrate faith into your busy life by looking for ways to serve others. Acts of kindness, whether large or small, are opportunities to live out your faith. Whether it's offering encouragement to a coworker, helping a neighbor, or volunteering your time, service becomes a powerful expression of God's love.

Deepening the Integration

To deepen this habit, consider developing a rule of life—a simple framework for how you want to live out your faith in all areas of life. This might include specific actions, like praying during meals, reading scripture in the morning, or seeking out regular fellowship with others. A rule of life helps you to be intentional about your spiritual practices and keeps your focus on God, no matter how busy your day gets.

Daily habits are the cornerstone of spiritual growth. By incorporating small but meaningful practices like reading a verse a day, practicing gratitude, listening to worship music or podcasts, and integrating faith into your busy life, you can cultivate a vibrant spiritual life that keeps you grounded, encouraged, and aligned with God's purpose. It's not about doing everything perfectly or making huge leaps in your faith all at once—it's about taking consistent, intentional steps toward growth each day.

As you develop these habits, you'll find that your spiritual life becomes more deeply embedded in the rhythms of your day, and your faith will grow stronger, more vibrant, and more alive.

Closing Prayer:

God, Thank You for fresh starts. Help the reader carry one habit from this chapter into real life—even if it's as simple as praying before scrolling. Turn routine into connection. And remind them: baby steps still move us forward. Amen.

Part 3: Overcoming Temptation

Chapter 7: Identifying Your Triggers

Opening Prayer:

Jesus, We're about to poke at some things. Help the reader resist the urge to say "I'm fine" and let You in instead. This might get weird, but You do good work in weird. Show them their triggers—not to shame, but to heal. Amen.

"The Battle of the Pants: A Tale of Temptation and Stretchy Waistbands"

It all started with a pair of jeans.

Not just any jeans—my favorite jeans. The kind that used to fit like they were tailored just for me. High-waisted. Flattering. Worn-in just right.

Then one morning, I went to put them on and they betrayed me.

I mean, really betrayed me.

I did the whole hop-shimmy-squat, then lay on the bed routine. Tried holding my breath like I was diving for pearls. Nothing worked. They stopped at the waist and said, "Absolutely not, ma'am."

Now, here's where things got spiritual. Because instead of just acknowledging I might need to lay off the afternoon cinnamon rolls, I launched into a full theological breakdown.

"Okay, Lord," I prayed dramatically in front of the mirror. "What is this temptation You speak of in Your Word? Is it... snacks? Is it emotional eating? Am I finding false comfort in frosted baked goods?"

Deep down, I already knew the answer.

Yes.

I was using food to self-soothe. You see, nearly two years ago, the company I worked for was sold, and the transition was overwhelming. I didn't just work there. My entire family did. The stress of the acquisition consumed everything. What made it even harder was that I had truly loved the previous owners—they weren't just colleagues, they had become family in the truest sense. My husband, Ben and I were particularly close to the owner's son. Our children married one another. We share a grandson with this man. The closeness we once had, even before our children fell in love, disappeared overnight.

My husband and I were left feeling discarded—like we no longer mattered once we were no longer useful. It hurt more than I can express. We didn't just lose a job; we lost people we deeply cared for, and a person who made us feel as if our friendship was transactional.

I still attend church with this man. I still share a family with him. I remember praying for him constantly when his father was ill (I still pray for him today), doing everything I could to support him, pouring my heart and time into being there. This was after knowing the company was to be sold. That fact changed nothing for me. My "job" as his friend was to be present in a way that reflected God's love in his time of need. But even before the company changed hands, the phone stopped ringing. The lunches, dinners, vacations together, the check-ins—gone.

He always said he was "just so busy." Maybe he was. Maybe he still is. Aren't we all? But it only takes a moment to check on someone who gave so much. You make time for people who are important to you, afterall, right? Did he not want to reflect God's love back? We were going through all-consuming stress and change, and he decided not to show up for us. I was angry, I was hurt, I was confused. Were we not as important to him as I believed us to be? That answer came in a clear, resounding silence.

I'll confess, y'all—my thumbs betrayed me. I sent that text. The kind of text that makes the Holy Spirit do a slow blink. It was part honesty, part sass, and fully fueled by feelings. I let him know he was acting like someone who needed a "Who Even Are You?" intervention. He was unrecognizable to us. I reminded him that we were hurting too, life was sprinting past us like it had somewhere to be, and we were just out here confused—like, "Hello? Did you get raptured early?"

And how did he respond? You guessed it. With the spiritual gift of ghosting. Again. Like he was trying out for the role of Casper but without the friendly part.

Eventually, I stopped trying. I stopped reaching out to someone who never reached back. I got tired of putting him in the position to make excuses, if he bothered to answer at all, as to why he can't do x, y, or z with us. I let go of the "brother" who no longer had time or space for us in his life. And that loss—that silent goodbye—has been one of the most painful parts of all, and one he hasn't noticed or missed.

Don't get me wrong—I wasn't binging entire cakes in secret. It was subtle. It was routine. A little "treat" here after a hard conversation. A little "reward" there for doing laundry. A midnight cookie because I was processing life.

But somewhere along the way, I'd developed a pattern. Bad day? Eat a brownie. Good day? Celebrate with nachos. Stress? Drive-thru.

I wasn't hungry. I was coping.

And the jeans were trying to tell me the truth.

So, I decided to get serious. Not about a diet—about discipline. I pulled out my notes, my Bible, and my comfiest sweatpants (because let's be realistic), and asked God to show me where my triggers were.

And oh, He delivered.

Within 24 hours I had:

- *Gotten irritated by a passive-aggressive email and immediately reached for a family-size bag of pretzels.*

- *Yelled at my dog far eating out of the cats litter box (again) and then opened the freezer for ice cream.*

- *Had a heartfelt emotional conversation with a friend, a non transactional friend, and somehow ended up in the Sonic drive-thru ordering a route 44 vanilla coke and cheese sticks—for the road.*

By the end of the week, I was seeing my pattern more clearly than ever.

The trigger wasn't food.

It was stress. Insecurity. Disappointment. Control.

And I had slowly, sneakily, trained myself to run to food instead of God.

So, I did what every good Christian does when they feel convicted: I made a plan.

I'd memorize Scripture. I'd journal my feelings. I'd drink water. And—this part was crucial—I'd stop buying snacks "for the kids" because, let's face it, the kids don't live here anymore. It's me. I'm the kid.

Day One: I felt powerful. Temptation came, and I quoted James 4:7 out loud. "Resist the devil, and he will flee from you!" I think even my dog looked impressed.

Day Two: I journaled through a craving and felt like a spiritual warrior. Who even needs chocolate when you have clarity and inner peace?

Day Three: I found myself staring longingly at a granola bar like it was the golden calf.

But I didn't eat it.

Instead, I prayed.

And y'all, it wasn't fancy. It was more like, "Jesus, please help me not destroy this snack like a biblical plague. Amen."

And slowly... it started to work.

Not perfectly. Not magically. But intentionally.

I noticed that temptation always came in the same outfit: stress, emotion, and silence.

So I started preloading my days with Scripture. I made playlists of worship songs. I practiced the holy art of taking a walk away from my desk when I felt like crumbling into temptation (and cookies).

And eventually, the jeans? They fit again.

But honestly, that became the least important part.

Because the real victory wasn't in the zipper. It was in the awareness.

I wasn't reacting on autopilot anymore. I was noticing. Pausing. Choosing.

I began to see how much of temptation is tied to ignoring your heart. When you don't know what you're feeling—or don't want to feel it— you'll reach for anything to numb it. And for me, that "anything" came in wrappers.

But God is better than a brownie. And grace tastes sweeter than any frosting.

One night, after a particularly stressful day, I opened my cabinet without thinking. My hand hovered over a cookie bag. I paused.

Then I closed the cabinet and whispered, "Not this time."

I walked into my bedroom, sat on the edge of the bed, and just said, "God, I'm tired. I'm overwhelmed. I feel invisible today. Be near."

And He was.

It wasn't dramatic. There were no angels or holy gusts of wind. But I felt seen. I felt like I'd finally chosen comfort that didn't leave me with crumbs and guilt.

Here's what I learned: overcoming temptation isn't about being strong.

It's about being aware.

It's about identifying your triggers and inviting God into the moment where the decision is made.

And sometimes? It's about choosing prayer over pretzels.

Temptation may wear different costumes for all of us—anger, gossip, overspending, resentment, TikTok binges, you name it. But the enemy's strategy is always the same: isolate, distract, and derail.

Our strategy?

Know your patterns.

Talk to God before the spiral.

Be honest about what you're actually craving.

And maybe, keep a few sticky notes on your fridge that say, "No eternal satisfaction found in here."

Because while jeans will stretch and shrink and betray you without warning, God stays constant.

He's the one Comfort that won't go straight to your hips.

Sin and temptation are universal struggles. Every believer, no matter how mature in their faith, faces moments of weakness, distraction, and vulnerability. One of the most powerful ways to grow in our spiritual walk and become more Christlike is to identify the triggers—those patterns or situations—that lead us to sin or temptation. These triggers don't just happen randomly. They often follow patterns and are rooted in deep, sometimes unconscious, responses to stress, emotions, or circumstances.

Understanding these triggers and learning how to manage them is essential for spiritual growth and emotional health. In this chapter, we'll explore how to recognize and address patterns that lead to sin and temptation. We'll also delve into eight practical tools that can help you achieve greater self-awareness, gain control over negative behaviors, and strengthen your ability to live in alignment with God's will.

By the end of this chapter, you'll have actionable steps to recognize your personal triggers, reflect on your own heart's condition, and take control over patterns that lead you away from God.

What Are Triggers?
Before we dive into the tools for identifying your triggers, let's first define what triggers are. In simple terms, triggers are the situations, people, emotions, or environments that lead to temptation, poor decision-making, or even outright sin. These might be conscious triggers, like a particular person or a stressful situation that tempts you to respond in anger, or they might be unconscious, like deep-seated fears or insecurities that lead you to engage in sinful behaviors as a way of coping.

Sin often doesn't happen in a vacuum. We don't just "slip" into sin without prior influences. It's important to understand that sin usually follows a process, starting with a trigger, leading to a response, and often resulting in a sinful action. By identifying the patterns that lead to sin in our lives, we can begin to make intentional choices to avoid those patterns and grow in Christlikeness.

James 1:14-15 teaches us about this process: "But each person is tempted when they are dragged away by their own evil desire and enticed. Then, after desire has conceived, it gives birth to sin; and sin, when it is full-grown, gives birth to death."

Understanding this process helps us see how important it is to identify the triggers early, before they lead to sinful behavior.

Why Identifying Triggers Matters

If we do not recognize the triggers that lead us into sin, we remain at the mercy of those patterns, continuously battling temptation without a real plan of action. But when we understand the root causes and patterns, we gain insight into our weaknesses and can actively take steps to prevent sinful responses. This kind of self-awareness is the key to living a victorious life in Christ.

Jesus, during His earthly ministry, warned His followers to be vigilant against temptation. In Matthew 26:41, He said, "Watch and pray so that you will not fall into temptation. The spirit is willing, but the flesh is weak."

Identifying triggers is an essential part of watching and praying, and it allows us to protect our hearts from sin before it takes root.

8 Tools for Identifying and Managing Your Triggers
1. Journaling for Reflection

As we already discussed in Chapter 4, Journaling can be a powerful and meaningful way to connect with God. Journaling is also a powerful tool for self-reflection. Writing down your thoughts, feelings, and experiences can help you identify patterns that may not be immediately obvious. When it comes to identifying your triggers, journaling allows you to record moments when you felt tempted or gave into sin. Over time, reviewing these entries can provide valuable insights into the situations or emotions that frequently lead you to sin.

In Psalm 139:23-24, David prays, "Search me, O God, and know my heart; test me and know my anxious thoughts. See if there is any offensive way in me, and lead me in the way everlasting." This verse can serve as a prayerful foundation for your journaling, inviting God to help you discover what might be hidden in your heart.

How to Use It:

- *Set aside time each day to journal about your experiences. Focus on moments where you felt tempted or emotionally charged.*
- *Record what happened leading up to the temptation. Was it a stressful situation? Did you interact with a particular person? Were you feeling lonely, insecure, or angry?*
- *Write about your feelings before, during, and after the event. This helps you identify emotional states that may contribute to your temptation.*
- *As you look back over your journal entries, look for repeating patterns. Do certain environments, interactions, or emotions consistently trigger certain sinful behaviors?*

The goal of journaling is not to condemn yourself but to gain clarity about what's really going on in your heart. By making this a regular practice, you'll grow in your self-awareness and begin to recognize early warning signs of temptation.

2. The "Pause" Technique

Sometimes, the key to identifying your triggers is learning to slow down. In moments of intense emotion or stress, our bodies tend to react before we have time to think. The "pause" technique encourages you to take a brief moment to stop and reflect before responding to a situation. This practice gives you the opportunity to identify whether the current situation is a trigger and how best to respond in alignment with your faith.

James 1:19-20 reminds us, "Everyone should be quick to listen, slow to speak and slow to become angry, because human anger does not produce the righteousness that God desires."

How to Use It:

- The next time you feel an emotional reaction (anger, frustration, lust, anxiety, etc.), pause before you act.
- Take a deep breath. Ask yourself, "What am I feeling right now? Why am I feeling this way?"
- Reflect briefly on what may have triggered the emotion. Are you responding to a past wound, a stressful situation, or a specific person?
- Decide, with God's help, how you want to respond. Pray for wisdom and strength to resist sin.

The "pause" technique is a way to interrupt the automatic emotional and behavioral patterns that often lead to sinful responses. By building the habit of pausing, you can allow the Holy Spirit to guide your thoughts and actions, rather than being driven by immediate emotional impulses.

3. Accountability Partnerships

Accountability is a critical component of spiritual growth and personal responsibility. Having someone you trust to walk with you in your faith journey provides the support and encouragement needed to recognize and address your triggers. An accountability partner can help you identify areas of weakness and hold you accountable when temptation strikes.

Ecclesiastes 4:9-10 states, "Two are better than one, because they have a good return for their labor: If either of them falls down, one can help the other up. But pity anyone who falls and has no one to help them up."

How to Use It:

- *Find someone you trust, whether a friend, mentor, or family member, who is committed to praying for you and holding you accountable.*
- *Share with them the specific triggers that you've identified in your life. Be open and honest about areas where you struggle.*
- *Ask them to pray for you and check in regularly to see how you're handling your triggers.*
- *When you experience a trigger, reach out to your accountability partner for prayer and guidance.*

The beauty of accountability is that it creates a safe space to confess, seek help, and grow together. It also helps to know that you're not alone in your struggles, and that someone is standing with you to pray for your victory over sin.

4. Cognitive Behavioral Tools (CBT)

Cognitive Behavioral Therapy (CBT) is a therapeutic technique that focuses on changing negative thought patterns to improve behavior. While CBT is typically used in clinical settings, its principles can be applied to spiritual growth by helping you identify and challenge unhelpful or sinful thought patterns. By replacing these thoughts with truth from Scripture, you can interrupt the cycle that leads to temptation.

Romans 12:2 teaches us, "Do not conform to the pattern of this world, but be transformed by the renewing of your mind. Then you will be able to test and approve what God's will is—his good, pleasing and perfect will."

How to Use It:

- *Start by recognizing when a negative or sinful thought enters your mind (e.g., "I'll never be good enough," or "I deserve to be angry").*

- *Pause and ask yourself: Is this thought based on truth? Does it align with what God says about me and my situation?*
- *Replace the negative thought with a truth from God's Word. For example, if you feel unworthy, remind yourself that you are accepted in Christ (Romans 8:1).*
- *Practice this whenever you recognize harmful thought patterns.*

By training your mind to replace negative or sinful thoughts with truth, you break the cycle of sin before it leads to action.

5. Setting Boundaries

Many times, triggers are associated with specific environments, relationships, or situations. Setting boundaries is a proactive way to protect yourself from falling into temptation. Boundaries help you determine what is acceptable in your life and what is not, and they provide a clear line that you refuse to cross.

Proverbs 4:23 reminds us, "Above all else, guard your heart, for everything you do flows from it."

How to Use It:

- *Identify areas in your life where you frequently fall into temptation (e.g., certain friendships, environments, or situations).*
- *Set clear boundaries to limit exposure to these triggers. For example, if you struggle with gossip, avoid conversations where gossip tends to flourish.*
- *Communicate your boundaries with others, and stick to them consistently.*
- *Remember that boundaries are not about avoiding people but about protecting your spiritual health.*

Boundaries are an act of self-control and self-care. They honor God by preserving your purity, integrity, and relationship with Him.

6. Prayer and Scripture Memorization

Prayer and Scripture memorization are two of the most powerful tools we have in the battle against temptation. Both enable us to fight temptation with God's truth and draw near to Him in times of weakness. When you're able to recite Scripture and pray in moments of temptation, you empower yourself to resist sin.

Psalm 119:11 says, "I have hidden your word in my heart that I might not sin against you."

How to Use It:

- *Identify Scriptures that speak to your specific struggles or triggers. For example, if you struggle with anger, memorize James 1:19-20: "Everyone should be quick to listen, slow to speak, and slow to become angry."*
- *Commit to daily prayer and Scripture reading, especially when you know you're prone to temptation.*
- *In moments of temptation, immediately pray and recite the Scriptures you've memorized.*

By consistently integrating prayer and Scripture into your routine, you create a spiritual arsenal that is readily available when you face triggers.

7. Mindfulness and Emotional Awareness

Sometimes, our triggers are tied to deep emotions that we haven't fully processed. Mindfulness helps you become more aware of your emotions and how they influence your behavior. By paying attention to how you feel, you can identify emotions that lead to sin and take steps to manage them before they escalate.

Philippians 4:6-7 encourages us, "Do not be anxious about anything, but in every situation, by prayer and petition, with thanksgiving, present your requests to God. And the peace of God, which transcends all understanding, will guard your hearts and your minds in Christ Jesus."

How to Use It:

- Practice mindfulness by regularly checking in with yourself throughout the day. Ask yourself, "What am I feeling right now? Why do I feel this way?"
- Identify emotions like fear, loneliness, insecurity, or anger that may lead to sinful reactions.
- Use this awareness to take proactive steps to process emotions in healthy ways, whether through prayer, journaling, or talking to someone you trust.

Mindfulness helps you become more emotionally intelligent and aware of the internal processes that lead to sinful behavior.

8. Spiritual Disciplines for Strengthening Faith

Finally, consistently engaging in spiritual disciplines—such as worship, fasting, or service—strengthens your faith and fortifies you against temptation. When you are spiritually grounded and connected to God, you are more equipped to handle life's challenges and temptations.

1 Timothy 4:7-8 reminds us, "Train yourself to be godly. For physical training is of some value, but godliness has value for all things, holding promise for both the present life and the life to come."

How to Use It:

- Commit to regular spiritual disciplines that help you grow in your relationship with God.
- Set aside time for daily Bible reading, prayer, and worship.

- *Serve others in your community to cultivate a heart of humility and obedience.*

Spiritual disciplines are essential for staying rooted in God's Word and strengthening your resolve against temptation.

Identifying and managing your triggers is essential for living a life that honors God. By using tools like journaling, prayer, mindfulness, and accountability, you can begin to recognize the patterns in your life that lead to sin and temptation. With these tools in hand, you can proactively address your triggers, replace negative thought patterns with God's truth, and live a life of victory in Christ.

Closing Prayer:

Lord, Thank You for the courage to look inward. For every lightbulb moment, sarcastic eye-roll, or "ugh, that's me" realization—thank You. Keep working gently and thoroughly. You're not trying to expose to embarrass—You expose to heal. Amen.

Chapter 8: Strategies for Avoiding and Overcoming Temptation

Opening Prayer:

God, Here's the thing: temptation is real and sometimes weirdly convenient. Please help this reader recognize when it's creeping in— and help them actually want Your way more than whatever the moment is offering. Also, thank You for not throwing lightning bolts when we mess up. Amen.

Temptation is one of the most challenging aspects of the Christian life. It is a universal struggle that no believer is exempt from. Jesus Himself faced temptation in the wilderness (Matthew 4:1-11), and He warned His disciples about the dangers of temptation (Matthew 26:41). However, God does not leave us without guidance or strength to overcome it. In fact, the Bible is full of practical strategies for avoiding and overcoming temptation, and we can find comfort and hope in knowing that we are not alone in this battle.

"Joseph vs. The HR Violation: A Modern Temptation Story"

Joseph had a good job. He started out in a rough spot—family drama, sold into a sketchy situation, you know how it is—but eventually, he landed a solid gig as the executive assistant to Potiphar, a powerful government official. Joseph was smart, good-looking (like, "Bible says so" level handsome), and totally trusted.

Enter Mrs. Potiphar. Let's just say she had a habit of forgetting boundaries.

Every day she'd find a reason to "accidentally" show up in Joseph's office with a "question about a spreadsheet"—even though she hadn't opened Excel since Pharaoh's first term.

> *"Joseph," she purred one day, "you work too hard. You deserve a little... break."*

Strategy #1: Avoidance

Joseph was like, "Oh no, I'm not even replying to that Slack message."
He literally started scheduling his breaks around her schedule. Took the long way around the palace. Pretended to be on Zoom calls just to avoid interaction.

Why? Because Joseph knew: the best way to beat temptation is often to not be in the room when it walks in wearing perfume and bad intentions.

Strategy #2: Accountability Partner

He didn't have texting back then, but if he did, Joseph would've been in a group chat called "Purity Bros" with Daniel and Job. Every day he probably sent something like,
> *"Pray for me. Mrs. P out here again with her weird shoulder shrugs."*
> *And they'd reply with prayer hands and a verse meme.*

Accountability isn't just confession—it's community. Joseph stayed grounded because he wasn't spiritually isolated.

Strategy #3: Prayer & Scripture

When Mrs. Potiphar really crossed the line and grabbed his robe, Joseph didn't give a long sermon. He ran. Left his coat. Saved his character.

But don't miss it: he'd already built up the inner strength to run. That kind of decision doesn't happen by accident. That's the result of knowing what's right, praying for strength daily, and letting God's truth shape your reflexes.

Joseph didn't just resist temptation—he sprinted past it like it was a burning building.

Moral of the story?

Temptation is not a maybe—it's a guarantee. But victory is possible when you practice:

- **Avoidance** *(don't play with fire)*

- **Accountability** *(walk with wise friends)*

- **Prayer & Scripture** *(keep your spiritual muscles strong)*

And remember: sometimes the holiest thing you can do… is leave your coat and run.

In this chapter, we will explore three powerful and practical strategies for overcoming temptation: **Avoidance**, **Accountability Partners**, *and* **Prayer and Scripture for Strength**. *Each of these strategies, when applied faithfully, can help us resist temptation and walk in victory.*

Strategy 1: Avoidance
Avoidance is a proactive strategy for resisting temptation. The Bible encourages us to be wise about the situations we place ourselves in and the environments we expose ourselves to. While we cannot escape every temptation, we can choose to avoid circumstances where we know we are most vulnerable. The principle of avoidance is about creating a safe space where we minimize exposure to situations, people, or things that trigger sin in our lives.

1. Avoidance of Tempting Situations

In 1 Corinthians 10:13, Paul encourages us: "No temptation has overtaken you except what is common to mankind. And God is faithful; He will not let you be tempted beyond what you can bear. But when you are tempted, He will also provide a way out so that you can endure it."

God, in His grace, provides a way out of temptation, but we are also called to be alert and avoid situations where temptation is more likely to occur. For instance, if you struggle with alcohol, avoiding places where drinking is the primary activity, like bars or certain social gatherings, would be wise. Similarly, if you struggle with lust, avoiding inappropriate media and online content can be a powerful measure of avoidance. We must ask ourselves, "Where am I most vulnerable to temptation, and what practical steps can I take to avoid those places?"

Consider the story of Joseph in Genesis 39. When Potiphar's wife tempted him to sin, Joseph didn't try to negotiate or reason with her. He fled. Genesis 39:12 says, "She caught him by his cloak and said, 'Come to bed with me!' But he left his cloak in her hand and ran out of the house."

Joseph's response is a powerful example of how avoidance works in the face of temptation. He didn't linger; he didn't try to resist by engaging in conversation. He simply ran away, sans his coat, from the situation. This act of avoidance spared him from sin and kept his heart pure.

2. Setting Boundaries and Guardrails

Setting boundaries is another form of avoidance that helps us maintain our integrity and resist temptation. Proverbs 4:23 says, "Above all else, guard your heart, for everything you do flows from it."

Boundaries help us guard our hearts by preventing us from entering situations where our emotions, desires, or weaknesses might get the best of us. These boundaries can be physical, relational, or even emotional. For example, if you struggle with gossip, setting boundaries in your conversations and distancing yourself from people who encourage gossip can help you avoid falling into that sin. In relationships, setting healthy boundaries in how you interact with others, especially in dating or friendships, can prevent you from crossing into areas of temptation.

Consider the story of David and Bathsheba (2 Samuel 11). David's failure to avoid temptation began when he stayed behind in Jerusalem while his men went to battle. He was in a vulnerable position, and it was in that moment that he saw Bathsheba bathing and gave in to temptation. David's failure to avoid the situation and set the boundary of not indulging in idle time led to a tragic sin that had long-lasting consequences. This story teaches us that avoiding idle situations and setting boundaries can be key to resisting temptation.

3. Avoiding Temptation Through Community

Another aspect of avoidance is surrounding ourselves with a strong, supportive community. The early church provides a great example of how believers can support one another in avoiding temptation. Acts 2:42-47 describes how the early Christians devoted themselves to fellowship, breaking bread, and supporting one another.

When we are connected to a community of believers, we can avoid temptations that arise from isolation or loneliness. Spending time with godly friends and mentors can help us stay accountable and avoid situations that might lead us astray. Fellowship in the body of Christ provides a source of encouragement and accountability, which is essential for resisting temptation.

Conclusion on Avoidance:

Avoidance isn't about running away from life or hiding from all challenges. It's about being wise and intentional in how we live our lives, choosing not to place ourselves in situations where we are vulnerable to temptation. Joseph's flight from temptation, David's failure to avoid temptation, and the example of the early church all demonstrate the importance of avoidance as a strategy for overcoming sin.

Strategy 2: Accountability Partners

Having an accountability partner is a powerful strategy for overcoming temptation. The Bible emphasizes the importance of community and mutual support among believers. In Ecclesiastes 4:9-10, we read, "Two are better than one, because they have a good return for their labor: If either of them falls down, one can help the other up. But pity anyone who falls and has no one to help them up."

Accountability partners provide support, encouragement, and correction when necessary. In the context of temptation, an accountability partner can help us recognize our weaknesses, pray with us, and hold us responsible for our actions.

1. Choosing the Right Accountability Partner

Not everyone is suited to be an accountability partner. You need someone who is trustworthy, spiritually mature, and committed to your well-being. Hebrews 10:24–25 says, "And let us consider how we may spur one another on toward love and good deeds, not giving up meeting together... but encouraging one another—and all the more as you see the Day approaching."

A good accountability partner should be someone who encourages you to grow in your faith, challenges you when necessary, and prays for you. They should also be someone who you feel comfortable being honest with, especially when it comes to your struggles with temptation. If you don't feel safe sharing your struggles with them, it's time to reassess the relationship.

2. The Role of Accountability in Overcoming Temptation

Having an accountability partner can help you stay focused and avoid falling into temptation. In Galatians 6:1-2, Paul writes, "Brothers and sisters, if someone is caught in a sin, you who live by the Spirit should restore that person gently. But watch yourselves, or you also may be tempted. Carry each other's burdens, and in this way you will fulfill the law of Christ."

Accountability isn't just about pointing out someone else's sins; it's about walking alongside one another in love and gentleness. When you share your struggles with an accountability partner, you are inviting them to help you carry the burden of temptation and sin. They can pray for you, provide godly counsel, and encourage you to keep going when the going gets tough.

One powerful example of accountability can be found in the life of David and Jonathan. In 1 Samuel 18:1-3, we see how David and Jonathan formed a deep bond of friendship and mutual support. Jonathan was there for David during some of his most challenging moments, offering guidance and encouragement. This type of relationship is a model for accountability, where both parties genuinely care for each other's spiritual growth and are willing to help each other stay on track.

3. Accountability and Transparency

To benefit from an accountability partnership, it's important to be transparent about your struggles and temptations. James 5:16 says, "Therefore confess your sins to each other and pray for each other so that you may be healed."

Confession isn't just about admitting wrongdoing; it's about bringing our weaknesses into the light so that others can pray with us and help us overcome. Transparency requires humility and vulnerability, but it also allows for healing and freedom from the weight of temptation.

A powerful example of this can be seen in the life of the Apostle Paul, who often shared his struggles with the churches he ministered to. In 2 Corinthians 12:9-10, Paul speaks about his "thorn in the flesh" and how he relied on God's grace to endure it. By sharing his struggles openly, Paul not only found strength in God but also showed others that they were not alone in their battles.

Conclusion on Accountability Partners:
Accountability is a crucial part of the Christian life and is vital in overcoming temptation. By choosing the right accountability partner, being transparent, and supporting one another in love, we can help each other resist temptation and grow in faith.

Strategy 3: Prayer and Scripture for Strength

The final strategy for overcoming temptation is prayer and the power of Scripture. Jesus Himself modeled the importance of prayer when He faced temptation in the wilderness. In Matthew 4:1-11, when Satan tempted Jesus, He responded each time with Scripture, demonstrating the power of God's Word in overcoming temptation.

1. Prayer as a Tool for Overcoming Temptation

Prayer is one of the most powerful weapons we have in resisting temptation. In Matthew 26:41, Jesus tells His disciples, "Watch and pray so that you will not fall into temptation. The spirit is willing, but the flesh is weak."

When we pray, we invite God's strength into our lives and acknowledge our dependence on Him. Prayer helps us stay connected to God, seek His guidance, and receive the power we need to resist temptation. In times of temptation, turning to God in prayer is an act of faith that reminds us we are not facing the battle alone.

2. Using Scripture as a Shield

The Bible is full of promises and truths that we can rely on when facing temptation. Jesus' use of Scripture during His time of temptation is a powerful example of how God's Word can be a shield against the lies of the enemy. When Jesus was tempted to turn stones into bread, He responded with Deuteronomy 8:3, "Man shall not live on bread alone, but on every word that comes from the mouth of God."

In times of temptation, it is crucial to have Scripture memorized and ready to use. Ephesians 6:17 describes the Word of God as the "sword of the Spirit," which is able to cut through lies and deceit. When you face temptation, speaking God's Word aloud can help you stand firm and resist.

3. Encouraging Stories of Overcoming

One of the most encouraging stories of overcoming temptation comes from the life of Billy Graham. He once shared in an interview that early in his ministry, he struggled with temptations of pride and sin. However, he made a decision to dedicate himself to prayer and Scripture reading daily, committing to never compromise his integrity. Through consistent prayer and reliance on God's Word, Billy Graham was able to overcome the temptations that came his way and continue his ministry with unwavering faithfulness.

Conclusion on Prayer and Scripture for Strength:

Prayer and Scripture are indispensable tools in the battle against temptation. Through prayer, we connect with God and receive His strength, and through Scripture, we gain the wisdom and truth necessary to fight off the lies of the enemy. When we combine prayer with the power of God's Word, we have everything we need to stand firm in the face of temptation.

Temptation will always be a part of the Christian journey, but with these strategies—Avoidance, Accountability Partners, and Prayer and Scripture for Strength—we are not left without hope. Through wisdom, community, and God's Word, we can resist temptation and live in the freedom that Christ has won for us. Remember, you are not alone in this battle. God is with you, and He will provide a way out of every temptation. Take heart and stand firm in His strength.

Closing Prayer:

Thank You, Lord, For being stronger than every temptation and kinder than we deserve when we fall. Help this reader leave this chapter with new tools, fresh grace, and maybe an accountability buddy who doesn't let them make late-night Amazon decisions (except of course, this book!). Amen.

Chapter 9: The Role of Community and Support

Opening Prayer:

God, Community sounds beautiful in theory, but sometimes people are weird, like me, and group texts are worse...especially when you type the quiet parts out that everyone was thinking anyway, but no one says because they don't want to seem weird...yeah Lord, you know that's also me. Still, we need each other. So I pray You help this reader find "their people." Real, Jesus-loving, casserole-sharing, prayer-saying humans. Even if it takes time. Amen.

The Christian faith is not meant to be lived in isolation. God designed us for community, and throughout Scripture, we are encouraged to live in fellowship with other believers. We see from the very beginning in Genesis 2:18 that "it is not good for man to be alone," and this principle holds true in our spiritual lives as well. From the early church, which was marked by deep communal relationships, to the individual letters written by the apostles, Scripture constantly emphasizes the importance of being surrounded by supportive, like-minded individuals who can walk alongside us in our faith journey.

In this chapter, we will explore the role of community and support in our Christian walk. We will discuss the importance of surrounding ourselves with individuals who share our values and faith, how our relationships with others shape our spiritual lives, and why finding the right faith community is crucial for growth and perseverance. With practical tips, we'll look at how to find a community that aligns with your personal values and lifestyle, and we will see how the Bible encourages us to be intentional about our relationships.

Why Community Matters: Biblical Foundations
"The Church-Hopper Chronicles: How I Found My People (Over and Over Again)"

If frequent flyer miles applied to church hunting, I'd have enough to fly direct to the gates of heaven.

In my adult life, I've moved close to a dozen times—across state lines, international borders, and at least three different climate zones (do not recommend moving from Canada to the subtropics with wool sweaters). With every move came a new favorite restaurant, new grocery store, new neighbors—and the ultimate quest: finding a new church family.

And to make things even more interesting, I'm an introvert by nature. I don't connect with others easily. Actually, if I were honest, most times I'd prefer not to connect at all. I'm not the type to walk into a room and start mingling like I'm running for church council president. I'm more likely to locate the nearest exit and overthink whether I said "God bless you" weirdly after someone sneezed.

You'd think by now I'd have this process down to a science. I do not.

One time, I showed up to a church that turned out to be a wedding. A literal wedding. I just thought they really liked love songs and formal wear.

Another time, I ended up in a house church that turned out to be more of a "let's read the Bible and also sell you protein powder" situation.

But through all the trial and error, one thing has become crystal clear: **we need each other.**

God didn't design faith to be a solo sport. We weren't meant to white-knuckle our way through life trying to follow Jesus on our own. That's like trying to assemble IKEA furniture without the manual and without the tiny hex key. You're gonna cry and probably break something.

Every time I moved, I had to start over—again. Walk into a church where I knew no one, force a smile, and try not to look like a lost puppy during worship. But you know what? God always brought people. Not perfect people, but my people. People who loved Jesus, who shared their testimonies and casseroles, and who reminded me I wasn't alone.

Those relationships shaped my walk more than any podcast or sermon ever could. They were the ones who checked on me when I was overwhelmed, prayed for me when I didn't even know how to pray, and made me laugh when I just wanted to quit adulting altogether.

The Bible's not subtle about this either. Hebrews 10:25 basically says, "Don't ghost your church family. You need them and they need you." (Okay, that's a paraphrase.)

So here's the practical part:
If you're looking for a faith community, start by asking what you actually need in this season. Big church or small? Quiet or lively? Doctrinally sound or just… soundproof? (Looking at you, drum-heavy worship teams.)

Then visit. Be awkward. Say hi. Linger awkwardly near the lobby. Follow up. It won't always be love at first pew, but if you're faithful, God is even more faithful.

Bottom line:
Faith is personal, but it's never meant to be private. The right community won't just help you grow—they'll help you stay when it gets hard.

Also, if they serve donuts, that helps too.

The Bible is clear that we are not meant to journey through life alone, especially in our walk with Christ. From the early church to the writings of Paul and other apostles, we see countless examples of the importance of relationships within the body of believers.

1. The Early Church as a Model for Community

The early Christians provided a powerful example of how believers should live together in community. In Acts 2:42-47, we read:

"They devoted themselves to the apostles' teaching and to fellowship, to the breaking of bread and to prayer. Everyone was filled with awe at the many wonders and signs performed by the apostles. All the believers were together and had everything in common. They sold property and possessions to give to anyone who had need. Every day they continued to meet together in the temple courts. They broke bread in their homes and ate together with glad and sincere hearts, praising God and enjoying the favor of all the people. And the Lord added to their number daily those who were being saved."

This passage reflects the depth of connection, mutual support, and commitment to one another that defined the early church. Believers were devoted to each other, shared their possessions, and gathered regularly to pray, worship, and study the Word. The Lord used this community to draw people to Himself, demonstrating the power of living out the gospel in relationships.

This communal model is foundational for us today. It shows that the Christian faith is about more than individual spirituality; it is about the collective journey of believers working together to encourage, support, and hold each other accountable.

2. The Power of Mutual Support and Accountability

The Bible also speaks to the importance of mutual support and accountability within a faith community. In Hebrews 10:24-25, the author encourages believers to:

"And let us consider how we may spur one another on toward love and good deeds, not giving up meeting together, as some are in the habit of doing, but encouraging one another—and all the more as you see the Day approaching."

Here, we see that the act of coming together isn't just for fellowship, but for encouragement and spurring one another on in our faith. This mutual accountability helps us grow spiritually and resist temptation. When we gather with fellow believers, we are reminded of God's faithfulness, encouraged to persevere, and strengthened to live out His calling in our lives.

This idea of mutual support is reflected in Romans 12:10–13, where Paul encourages us to, "Be devoted to one another in love. Honor one another above yourselves. Share with the Lord's people who are in need. Practice hospitality."

Community allows us to share the weight of life's challenges, whether they are personal struggles, emotional burdens, or spiritual battles. When we carry each other's burdens, we create a bond of love and support that helps us grow stronger in our faith.

3. The Influence of Our Relationships

The people we surround ourselves with can have a profound impact on our spiritual lives. Proverbs 13:20 states, "Walk with the wise and become wise, for a companion of fools suffers harm."

This verse highlights the importance of choosing our companions carefully. Those we spend time with shape our values, behaviors, and attitudes. The people we allow into our lives either encourage us toward Christ or draw us away from Him. If we surround ourselves with wise, godly individuals, we are more likely to grow in wisdom and faith. On the other hand, spending time with individuals who do not share our values or who lead us away from Christ can hinder our spiritual growth.

The principle of "birds of a feather flock together" is deeply rooted in this biblical teaching. Our relationships matter because they either elevate or hinder our faith. Proverbs 27:17 reinforces this idea: "As iron sharpens iron, so one person sharpens another."

When we choose to walk with those who are pursuing the same goals—faith in Christ, holiness, and spiritual growth—we strengthen one another. Together, we grow sharper and more focused on Christ, helping each other overcome the obstacles and temptations that arise in life.

The Importance of Finding the Right Faith Community

When it comes to finding the right faith community, there are several factors to consider. A strong community is one that aligns with your personal values, lifestyle, and spiritual goals. The right community will help you grow in your faith, keep you accountable, and encourage you in your walk with Christ.

But how do you find a community that truly fits? How can you ensure that you are surrounding yourself with the right people? Here are six practical tips for finding a faith community that aligns with your values and lifestyle:

1. Know Your Core Beliefs and Values

Before you can find a community that aligns with your beliefs, it is important to know what those beliefs are. Take time to reflect on the core principles of your faith—things like your views on salvation, the authority of Scripture, the nature of God, and how you view the Church. Having a clear understanding of what you believe will help you identify communities that align with your values.

Matthew 7:24-25 encourages us to build our lives on a strong foundation: "Therefore everyone who hears these words of mine and puts them into practice is like a wise man who built his house on the rock. The rain came down, the streams rose, and the winds blew and beat against that house; yet it did not fall, because it had its foundation on the rock."

When you have a strong foundation of faith, you can more easily identify a community that will help you stay rooted in the truth of God's Word.

2. Seek Out Churches with Sound Doctrine

When looking for a faith community, it is essential to ensure that the church or group adheres to sound biblical doctrine. In 1 Timothy 4:16, Paul writes to Timothy, "Watch your life and doctrine closely. Persevere in them, because if you do, you will save both yourself and your hearers."

Sound doctrine is essential because it keeps believers grounded in the truth of Scripture. Look for a church or group that preaches the gospel faithfully, teaches from the Bible, and upholds the centrality of Christ. A community that is rooted in the Word of God will help you grow spiritually and avoid the pitfalls of false teaching.

3. Look for a Community that Encourages Holiness and Growth

A faith community should not only teach sound doctrine, but also encourage you to live out your faith in practical ways. In 1 Thessalonians 5:11, Paul writes, "Therefore encourage one another and build each other up, just as in fact you are doing."

This encouragement isn't just about providing comfort; it is about spurring one another on toward holiness and spiritual maturity. A strong faith community will challenge you to grow in your relationship with Christ, pursue personal holiness, and live out the gospel in everyday life.

Look for a community that offers opportunities for discipleship, spiritual growth, and accountability. Whether through small groups, Bible studies, or other programs, seek a community that provides avenues for you to grow in your faith and hold you accountable to your commitment to Christ.

4. Evaluate the Health of Relationships within the Community

A healthy faith community is one where members love and support one another. Jesus commands His followers to love one another as He has loved them (John 13:34-35). When you join a community, take note of how people treat each other. Are there deep, authentic relationships? Is there a spirit of love, kindness, and grace? Or do you notice division, gossip, or a lack of genuine care for one another?

1 Corinthians 13:4-7 gives us a picture of love in action: "Love is patient, love is kind. It does not envy, it does not boast, it is not proud. It does not dishonor others, it is not self-seeking, it is not easily angered, it keeps no record of wrongs. Love does not delight in evil but rejoices with the truth. It always protects, always trusts, always hopes, always perseveres."

Look for a community where love is evident in both words and actions. A loving community will support you through difficult times, encourage you in your walk with Christ, and help you grow in your faith.

5. Attend Services and Events Regularly

Sometimes, the best way to get a feel for a faith community is by attending services and events regularly. This will give you a sense of the culture of the church or group and how it aligns with your personal values and lifestyle. Attend a few services, participate in community events, and observe the dynamics between members. This can help you discern whether or not this is the right community for you.

Hebrews 10:25 encourages us not to neglect gathering together: "Not giving up meeting together, as some are in the habit of doing, but encouraging one another—and all the more as you see the Day approaching."

Regular participation in a church or faith community will help you build connections and determine whether the community is a good fit for you.

6. Engage and Serve

Finally, an essential part of finding the right community is being an active participant in it. Engage with others, build relationships, and look for ways to serve. The body of Christ is made up of many members, each with different gifts and talents, and every believer has something to contribute. When you serve others, you not only bless them, but you also experience the joy and fulfillment that comes from being part of something bigger than yourself.

1 Peter 4:10 encourages us: "Each of you should use whatever gift you have received to serve others, as faithful stewards of God's grace in its various forms."

Look for ways to contribute to the life of the community—whether through volunteering, serving in ministry, or simply offering support to those in need. Serving others will help you grow in your faith and deepen your relationships within the community.

Community is essential for spiritual growth, perseverance, and living out our faith. Surrounding ourselves with like-minded, supportive believers helps us grow in love, accountability, and wisdom. By finding a faith community that aligns with your personal values, beliefs, and lifestyle, you create an environment where you can thrive spiritually and walk faithfully with Christ.

As you seek out this community, remember that it's not just about finding a place to belong; it's about engaging in a relationship with others who are committed to growing in their faith and pursuing God together. Through intentional relationships, mutual encouragement, and the strength of community, you can overcome challenges, grow spiritually, and fulfill the calling that God has placed

Closing Prayer:

Thank You, God, For designing us for community—even if it's awkward at first. Help this reader not give up on finding their tribe. Bless them with a circle that cheers, prays, and calls them out with love and snacks. Amen.

Part 4: Living Faithfully Every Day

Chapter 10: Imperfect but Loved

Opening Prayer:

Jesus, This might be the chapter where the perfectionists squirm. Please help this reader unclench their spiritual jaw and breathe. Remind them that perfection was never the goal—grace was. Thank You for using cracked pots, awkward prayers, and over-thinkers like us. Amen.

Introduction

In a world that often values perfection, it's easy to feel discouraged when we fall short. The pursuit of flawlessness in our relationships, our work, and even in our spiritual lives can feel like an unattainable goal. Yet, throughout Scripture, we see that perfection is never the expectation God has for us. What He desires is a sincere, authentic relationship with Him, one that is marked by humility, dependence on His grace, and a willingness to grow. The beauty of God's love is that despite our imperfections, He still chooses to love us, use us, and transform us for His purposes. This chapter will explore the concept of being "imperfect but loved," diving into the reality that God's grace is sufficient for us, and His plan for our lives is not thwarted by our flaws.

We will look at examples from the Bible of people who struggled, failed, and were imperfect in many ways—but who were still loved and used mightily by God. These figures remind us that we do not have to be perfect to be part of God's kingdom. Our faith, though imperfect, is still precious to Him.

Perfection is Not the Goal—A Sincere Relationship with God Is

"Moses and the Bluetooth Bush: God Calls the Undeniably Unqualified"

Moses wasn't exactly in the prime of his life.

He was living in the middle of nowhere, working for his father-in-law (which, let's be honest, is humbling enough), and watching sheep like a guy who'd officially peaked at "wilderness intern." This was not a man crushing goals on LinkedIn. He didn't even have LinkedIn. He had dust. And sheep. And sandals with questionable arch support.

Now remember, Moses had a past. He'd once been a prince in Egypt, with the best of everything—education, wealth, eyeliner probably. But a little incident involving anger management and a dead Egyptian sent him fleeing into the desert faster than you can say "Pharaoh's gonna kill me."

So here he is, years later, in the wilderness, just trying to keep sheep from licking rocks, when suddenly—boom—a bush bursts into flames. Which is already concerning. But then... the bush talks.

Let's pause here.

If this were a modern story, Moses would've assumed he was dehydrated, or had accidentally ingested a wild mushroom. Or maybe his Bluetooth earbuds glitched and connected to someone else's audiobook. But no—it was God. Calling. Audibly. From a plant.

God says, essentially:

> *"Moses, I've got a mission for you. I want you to go back to Egypt and free My people."*

And Moses responds with the spiritual equivalent of:

> *"I think You've got the wrong guy. I can barely order Starbucks without stuttering."*

He starts rattling off excuses like a nervous teen explaining a bad report card:

- *"Who am I to do that?"*

- *"What if they don't believe me?"*

- *"I'm not good with words. Like... really not."*

- *"Can't You just send literally anyone else?"*

This is the man God picked to lead a nation.

He wasn't charismatic. He wasn't confident. He wasn't Insta-ready with a ring light and a leadership podcast. He was a flawed, fearful, self-doubting shepherd with a speech impediment.

And God still said, "Yep. That's My guy."

Why? Because God isn't looking for perfection—He's looking for obedience. He's not impressed with your resume. He wants your yes.

Moses eventually says yes (after God gets a little firm), and sure enough, God uses this hesitant, insecure man to perform miracles, lead millions, part the Red Sea, and deliver the Ten Commandments.

But it all started at a bush, with Moses feeling wildly underqualified.

Sound familiar?

How many of us hear God calling us to do something—serve, speak, start, forgive—and our first response is, "I'm not ready"?

We think we have to be polished, prepared, and practically perfect before God can use us. We think if our spiritual life doesn't look like a devotional cover—complete with latte art and soft lighting—God's probably disappointed.

But spoiler: He already knows your weaknesses. And He still calls you.

God doesn't use us in spite of our imperfections—He often uses us through them.

Moses didn't suddenly become eloquent or brave overnight. He still messed up. He still got overwhelmed. At one point he even broke the original Ten Commandments—literally shattered them like a toddler with a tablet. But God kept showing up.

Because what mattered wasn't Moses' perfection. It was his persistence. His presence. His eventual yes.

So here's the takeaway:

If you're waiting to feel ready, polished, and flawless before stepping into what God has for you—you'll be waiting forever. And also missing the burning bush right in front of you.

God isn't calling you because you're the best option. He's calling you because He loves working with people who know they need Him.

So whether you're a wilderness-dweller, a people-pleaser, or a perfectionist still rehearsing the "what if I fail" speech—hear this:

God isn't looking for the most impressive.
He's looking for the most available.

Moses' modern-day version?
Probably someone in Crocs, holding a half-drunk coffee, looking around like, "Are You sure You meant to call me?"

And God saying, "Yes. You. The mess with the mustard stain. Let's do this!"

God's expectation of us is not that we achieve perfection but that we pursue a relationship with Him that is genuine, humble, and responsive to His love. In fact, Scripture is clear that God's power is made perfect in our weakness. As Paul writes in 2 Corinthians 12:9, "But he said to me, 'My grace is sufficient for you, for my power is made perfect in weakness.' Therefore I will boast all the more gladly of my weaknesses, so that the power of Christ may rest upon me."

This verse underscores a profound truth: our imperfections are not a barrier to God's love or purpose for our lives. Instead, it is in our weakness that God's strength is most evident. When we acknowledge our need for Him, when we recognize our inability to live perfectly, we open the door for God to work powerfully in and through us.

Psalm 103:13-14 gives us another beautiful reminder of God's heart toward us:

"As a father shows compassion to his children, so the Lord shows compassion to those who fear him. For he knows our frame; he remembers that we are dust."

God knows that we are frail, that we are imperfect. And yet, He still loves us deeply. His compassion is not based on our ability to perform but on His deep love for us as His children. This is the foundation of the relationship He desires with us—a relationship rooted in grace, not perfection.

Biblical Figures Who Struggled But Were Loved and Used by God

As we explore the lives of biblical figures who struggled but were loved by God, we will see a pattern: each of them faced failures, weaknesses, or challenges, yet they were still chosen by God for great purposes. These individuals show us that even in our imperfections, God can still use us for His glory.

1. Moses: A Reluctant Leader

Moses is one of the most significant figures in the Bible. Yet, his journey to becoming a great leader was not without struggle. He was raised in Pharaoh's household but fled Egypt after killing an Egyptian guard (Exodus 2:11-15). When God called him to lead the Israelites out of slavery, Moses hesitated, doubting his ability and feeling inadequate. The "can you send literally anyone else" guy. In Exodus 3:11, Moses said, "Who am I that I should go to Pharaoh and bring the Israelites out of Egypt?" He even questioned God's call, citing his lack of eloquence in speech (Exodus 4:10). Despite his flaws, Moses obeyed God, and through him, God performed mighty miracles, leading the Israelites to freedom.

Moses' story reminds us that God doesn't call the perfect; He calls those who are willing to trust in His strength. Even when we feel inadequate or unworthy, God can still use us for His purposes.

2. David: A Man After God's Own Heart

David is often remembered as a man "after God's own heart" (Acts 13:22), yet his life was marked by significant moral failures. He committed adultery with Bathsheba and arranged for the death of her husband, Uriah (2 Samuel 11). Despite these grievous sins, David repented, and God forgave him. In Psalm 51, David pours out his heart to God, acknowledging his sin and asking for God's mercy: "Create in me a pure heart, O God, and renew a steadfast spirit within me" (Psalm 51:10).

David's story shows us that God's grace is greater than our failures. No matter how deeply we fall, God offers forgiveness and the opportunity for restoration. David's willingness to turn back to God, even after his failures, was a key reason why God continued to use him.

3. Jonah: A Prophet Who Tried to Run from God

Jonah is a classic example of someone who tried to run from God's call. God sent Jonah to the city of Nineveh to call its people to repentance, but Jonah, displeased with God's plan, fled in the opposite direction (Jonah 1:1-3). After being swallowed by a great fish and spending three days in its belly, Jonah finally obeyed God's command and went to Nineveh. Despite his reluctance and initial disobedience, God used Jonah to bring about a great spiritual revival in the city.

Jonah's story is a reminder that our struggles and even our resistance to God's will do not disqualify us from His love or purpose. God is sovereign, and He can work through even our reluctance to accomplish His plans.

4. Peter: A Disciple Who Denied Christ

Peter, one of Jesus' closest disciples, experienced a dramatic failure when he denied Jesus three times on the night of His arrest (Luke 22:61). Yet, despite Peter's denial, Jesus later restored him with a powerful call to ministry. In John 21:15-17, after Jesus' resurrection, He asks Peter three times, "Do you love me?" Peter affirms his love, and Jesus commissions him to "feed my sheep."

Peter's story highlights the deep grace of God. Even when we fail Him, Jesus reaches out to restore us, offering us a fresh start and a purpose. Like Peter, we are never beyond the reach of God's love.

5. Sarah: A Woman Who Laughed at God's Promise

Sarah, the wife of Abraham, laughed when God promised that she would have a son in her old age (Genesis 18:12-14). Sarah's doubt and laughter were rooted in her inability to see how such a promise could come to fruition. However, God's promise was not dependent on Sarah's belief in her own ability but on His power. Sarah went on to give birth to Isaac, and through him, God's covenant promise was fulfilled.

Sarah's story teaches us that even when we doubt God's promises, His plan is not thwarted by our lack of faith. He remains faithful, even when we struggle to trust Him.

6. Jacob: A Deceiver Transformed by God

Jacob was known for his deceitfulness—he tricked his brother Esau out of his birthright (Genesis 25:29-34) and deceived their father Isaac to steal Esau's blessing (Genesis 27). Yet, God still chose to work through Jacob. After wrestling with God, Jacob's name was changed to Israel, and he became the father of the twelve tribes of Israel (Genesis 32:28). Despite his past failures, Jacob became a key figure in God's redemptive plan.

Jacob's story is a testament to God's transforming power. No matter how we have sinned, God can change us and use us for His glory.

7. Rahab: A Prostitute Who Protected God's People

Rahab, a woman living in the city of Jericho, was a prostitute, but she demonstrated great faith when she hid the Israelite spies and helped them escape (Joshua 2:1-21). Rahab's actions saved her family, and she is later listed in the genealogy of Jesus (Matthew 1:5). Despite her past, Rahab became an ancestor of the Savior of the world. Rahab's story is an example of how God uses people from all walks of life, even those with a questionable past, for His purposes. God's love and grace are not limited by our past mistakes.

8. Gideon: A Reluctant Leader Who Led Israel to Victory

Gideon is introduced in the book of Judges as a man who was hiding in a winepress, fearful of the Midianites (Judges 6:11-12). When God called him to deliver Israel, Gideon doubted his ability and asked for signs to confirm God's will (Judges 6:36-40). Despite his hesitations, Gideon obeyed and led Israel to victory over their enemies. His story demonstrates that God can use even the most unlikely and fearful individuals to accomplish His will.

Gideon's life shows that God's strength is made perfect in our weakness. He can take our doubts and fears and use them to fulfill His purposes.

9. Thomas: A Doubter Who Became a Believer

Thomas, one of Jesus' twelve disciples, is often remembered for his doubt. After Jesus' resurrection, Thomas refused to believe that Jesus had risen until he could see the wounds in Jesus' hands and side (John 20:24-29). When Jesus appeared to him, Thomas declared, "My Lord and my God!" (John 20:28). Jesus gently rebuked Thomas, saying, "Blessed are those who have not seen and yet have believed."

Thomas's story reminds us that doubt is not the end of our faith journey. Even in our moments of questioning, God patiently draws us closer to Himself, leading us to deeper belief.

10. The Prodigal Son: A Wayward Son Who Was Welcomed Home

I know. I know. I've written of the Prodigal Son before. What can I say? It's one of my favorite biblical teachings. We may not all directly relate to Rahab or King David, but we all can relate to the Prodigal Son. The parable of the Prodigal Son (Luke 15:11-32) illustrates the depth of God's love and grace. The younger son demanded his inheritance and squandered it in reckless living. Yet, when he returned in repentance, his father ran to meet him with open arms, and probably steak, forgiving him and celebrating his return. The story reflects the unconditional love of God for those who have gone astray but return to Him.

The Prodigal Son's story is a powerful reminder that no matter how far we may stray from God, His love for us remains constant. He is always ready to welcome us home with grace and forgiveness.

These biblical figures—Moses, David, Jonah, Peter, Sarah, Jacob, Rahab, Gideon, Thomas, and the Prodigal Son—demonstrate that perfection is not the goal. They struggled, doubted, and failed in significant ways, but through their imperfections, they experienced God's love, grace, and faithfulness. Each of their stories speaks to the truth that God is not looking for perfect people; He is looking for those who are willing to turn to Him in their imperfection and receive His love and forgiveness.

God's love is not based on our performance but on His character. Our imperfections do not disqualify us from being used by Him. Instead, they provide an opportunity for His grace to shine through. Like these biblical figures, we, too, can be imperfect but loved—and in that love, we are invited to walk in relationship with a God who redeems, restores, and transforms.

The Bible makes it abundantly clear that no one is perfect. Even the most revered heroes of faith had flaws, made mistakes, and struggled with sin. This truth should bring great comfort to us. God doesn't call us to perfection; He calls us to Himself. He desires for us to be in a genuine, humble relationship with Him, one that is not based on our ability to meet the standards of the world or even our own standards but on His love and grace.

The reality is that everyone is flawed—no one is exempt. Even if someone's life appears perfect on the outside, behind closed doors, they, too, experience struggles and setbacks.

Perfection Is Not the Goal; A Sincere Relationship with God Is

Scripture is clear that our walk with God is not about being perfect. It's about being humble, authentic, and surrendered to His will. Consider Romans 3:23, "For all have sinned and fall short of the glory of God."

No one is exempt from sin. It doesn't matter how successful we appear or how "together" our lives may seem. We all struggle, we all fall short, and yet God loves us deeply. The beauty of God's grace is that He doesn't require us to be perfect in order to be loved and used. He simply calls us to come to Him as we are, with our brokenness and flaws, and allow His love to transform us.

Jesus Himself acknowledged this in Matthew 9:12-13, when He said, "It is not the healthy who need a doctor, but the sick. But go and learn what this means: 'I desire mercy, not sacrifice.' For I have not come to call the righteous, but sinners." Jesus came for those who are aware of their need for healing, not for those who think they have it all figured out.

The apostle Paul echoes this truth in 2 Corinthians 12:9, where God tells him, "But he said to me, 'My grace is sufficient for you, for my power is made perfect in weakness.' Therefore I will boast all the more gladly of my weaknesses, so that the power of Christ may rest upon me." It is in our weaknesses, our struggles, and our imperfections that God's power shines most brightly.

Everyone is Flawed – Even Those Who Appear Perfect

In our world today, it is easy to feel like everyone else has it all together. Social media, glossy magazine covers, and polished public personas make it seem like there are people out there who are flawless in every way. However, the truth is that everyone—without exception—is flawed. Every one of us faces struggles, battles sin, and deals with imperfections.

Take, for example, someone like Charles Spurgeon. Widely regarded as one of the greatest preachers in Christian history, Spurgeon was known for his deep theological insights and powerful sermons. But behind his public success, Spurgeon struggled with depression and physical ailments throughout his life. Despite his personal battles, Spurgeon maintained a passionate relationship with God, and his ministry has impacted countless lives.

Spurgeon himself acknowledged his struggles, stating, "I have learned to kiss the wave that throws me against the Rock of Ages." He understood that his imperfections and struggles, far from disqualifying him, drew him closer to God. His faithfulness in the face of hardship is a powerful reminder that God uses imperfect people for His purposes.

This example is not isolated. Throughout history, many Christians who have been seen as "giants of the faith" have faced deep personal struggles. Their lives demonstrate that God does not require perfection; He desires sincerity and faithfulness in the midst of imperfection.

Embracing God's Imperfect Love

Though only ten are listed here, every single biblical human, except One, struggled with imperfections, but all were loved and used by God. From Abraham's moments of fear to Samson's moral failures, from Rahab's sinful past to Thomas's doubts, and Elijah's despair, these biblical figures show us that God uses people who are not perfect by any means. And yet, despite their flaws, God loved them deeply and fulfilled His purposes through them.

The same is true for us today. Our imperfections, our struggles, and our failures do not disqualify us from God's love or His plan for our lives. Just as He used the imperfect lives of biblical figures to advance His kingdom, He can use us, too. In fact, it is often through our imperfections that God's grace and power are most clearly displayed.

We do not have to be perfect to be loved by God, nor do we have to be perfect to be used by Him. What God desires is a sincere, authentic relationship with us. As we come to Him in humility, acknowledging our flaws and our need for His grace, He meets us with open arms, ready to forgive, restore, and use us for His glory.

So, remember: perfection is not the goal. A sincere relationship with God is. In His love, we are accepted as we are—imperfect but deeply loved. And in that love, He equips us to fulfill the purposes He has for our lives. How will you let Him use you today?

Closing Prayer:

Lord, Perfection is exhausting. Thank You for not asking for it. Bless this reader with the freedom to show up imperfect but sincere. You never asked us to be flawless—just faithful. Amen.

Chapter 11: Serving God in Everyday Life

Opening Prayer:

God, Help this reader realize that You can use their ordinary actions to reflect extraordinary love. Whether it's holding the door, holding their tongue, or holding their peace in a meeting—they can shine for You. Small things matter. Amen.

"Apparently, Taking Out the Trash Counts as Ministry"

So here's what I've realized, and I say this with love and just a pinch of sarcasm: Somewhere along the way, we got this idea that serving God has to be some big, bold, Instagrammable thing. Like, if you're not leading a revival in a stadium or drilling wells in a remote village with one hand while preaching with the other, you're not "really" serving the Lord.

But let me tell you what I think: if that's the standard, 98% of us are failing—spectacularly.

I mean, bless those who are out there doing the Big Kingdom Work™. We need them. Seriously. But most of us? We're doing things like going to work, microwaving leftovers, trying to remember if we already put detergent in the washer, and praying our kids don't bring home lice again. And in all that chaos, it's really easy to think, "Well, I guess I'm just living my life, not really doing anything 'spiritual.'"

But that's wrong.

Because according to Scripture—and I've checked—God is a big fan of the small stuff. He's the same God who noticed the widow's tiny offering, who appreciated a cup of cold water given in His name, and who literally fed thousands of people with a child's Lunchable.

So yes, I've decided that God is 100% present in the "mundane." You can absolutely serve God while folding socks. (Even the mismatched ones. Especially the mismatched ones.)

Here's the deal: we tend to separate our lives into two categories—
"God stuff" and "everything else." Church on Sunday? God stuff.
Sharing a verse on Facebook? God stuff. Running late for work and
resisting the urge to honk at the guy who still doesn't understand
four-way stops? Not God stuff.

But what if it is?

What if being kind in traffic is ministry? (A convicting thought, I
know.)
What if responding to a rude email with grace instead of sarcasm is
you shining Jesus?
What if the most holy thing you do all day is choose not to lose it when
someone comes into your office to complain about the printer not
working, again?

We love to romanticize ministry. We picture spiritual giants doing
dramatic, world-changing things. And that's awesome. But I think
heaven throws a party every time a parent prays over their kid's day
while packing lunches, or a tired teacher shows up for another round of
chaos with grace, or someone at work chooses integrity even when it's
invisible.

That's ministry. That's service. And that's what God meant when He
said, "Whatever you do, do it all for the glory of God" (1 Corinthians
10:31). He didn't say, "Only the stuff that's impressive." He said
whatever. If you're breathing and doing something—anything—with
love and faithfulness, God sees it. And He calls it good.

So no, you don't have to lead a small group, launch a nonprofit, or
start a YouTube devotional series to serve the Lord. (Though if you do,
go off, just please fix your audio.) But most of the time, it's not about
doing something new—it's about doing the things you're already
doing, with God in mind.

Your office? It's a mission field.
Your kitchen? Sacred ground.
Your calendar? A place to practice faithfulness, not just productivity.

And yes, your hallway conversations, text messages, and group chats are all opportunities to either reflect Christ or… not.

It's funny, because we think, "Well, God's not really using me right now." Meanwhile, we're surrounded by people who are hurting, lonely, stressed, or just one kind word away from not spiraling that day. And we know these people! They're our coworkers, our friends, our neighbors, the tired-looking lady in line behind us at Wal-Mart who just muttered something about coupons and judgment day.

All of those moments matter.

And here's the kicker: it's not about getting it perfect. God's not watching your day like a divine TSA agent with a clipboard. He's not deducting points when your "Jesus smile" turns into a death stare in the preschool pickup line. He's watching for your heart. For your willingness. For those small acts of faithfulness that no one else sees.

So yes, I'm saying that taking out the trash without complaining? That might be one of the most spiritually mature things you do today.

In fact, the next time you're elbow-deep in dishes or in a meeting that should've been an email, just whisper to yourself: "This is ministry." Not because it's glamorous, but because it's faithful.

And if someone asks you what you're up to these days, you can confidently say,
"Oh, just over here serving the Lord in the sacred ministry of grocery store parking lots and drink refills."

Because every moment really is an opportunity to serve Him.

Even the weird ones. Especially the weird ones.

In the hustle and bustle of daily life, it's easy to forget that every moment is an opportunity to serve God. Often, we think that serving God is something reserved for the "big" moments—leading a church ministry, going on a mission trip, or preaching in front of a congregation. But the truth is, we can serve God in the everyday actions of life, in the small, seemingly mundane moments where we reflect His love to those around us. Whether in our homes, workplaces, schools, or neighborhoods, God calls us to live out our faith in practical ways that reflect His love to others.

This chapter will explore how to serve God in the everyday moments, with a focus on small but impactful acts of service. We will examine practical ways to reflect God's love, including through acts of kindness, being a light in challenging environments, and engaging in simple acts of service. We will also explore how historical figures demonstrated Christ's love through their actions and how we, too, can live out our faith through these examples.

Practical Ways to Reflect God's Love in Daily Actions

1. Acts of Kindness

Acts of kindness may seem like small gestures, but they have the power to deeply impact the lives of others. In fact, kindness is one of the most direct ways to show God's love. Jesus said in John 13:35, "By this everyone will know that you are my disciples, if you love one another."

Acts of kindness are an outward expression of our inward love for others. When we extend kindness to those around us, we reflect the heart of God. Let's look at five historical figures who demonstrated Christ's love through acts of kindness and how we can do the same.

1. Mother Teresa: A Life Devoted to the Poor

Mother Teresa is known worldwide for her tireless work among the poor and sick in Calcutta, India. She believed that kindness was a powerful form of service, no matter how small the act. She once said, "Not all of us can do great things. But we can do small things with great love."

Her life was marked by countless acts of kindness, from feeding the hungry to comforting the dying. Her deep love for the marginalized and destitute was a clear reflection of Christ's love for the poor.

How You Can Reflect God's Love:

- *Volunteer at a food bank or soup kitchen to help those in need.*
- *Donate gently used clothing to shelters.*
- *Offer to run errands or help with chores for a neighbor who is struggling.*

2. Florence Nightingale: Bringing Compassion to Nursing

Florence Nightingale, the founder of modern nursing, revolutionized healthcare in the 19th century. During the Crimean War, she served as a nurse, caring for wounded soldiers in harsh conditions. Known for her compassion and attention to detail, Nightingale treated each patient with dignity and love. Her work wasn't just about providing medical care; it was about showing people that they were valuable and worthy of love.

How You Can Reflect God's Love:

- *Volunteer at a hospital, nursing home, or hospice center.*
- *Take time to listen to someone who is going through a difficult time, offering them empathy and support.*
- *Take meals to the sick or those recovering from surgery.*

3. Dietrich Bonhoeffer: Standing Up for Justice

Dietrich Bonhoeffer was a German pastor and theologian who stood against the atrocities of Nazi Germany. He risked his life to help Jewish families escape the Holocaust and took part in efforts to resist Adolf Hitler's regime. Bonhoeffer's commitment to justice, even at great personal cost, reflected Christ's love for the oppressed.

How You Can Reflect God's Love:

- *Stand up for the voiceless, whether that's speaking out against abortion or other injustice or volunteering for organizations that fight human trafficking.*
- *Support local charities that work with orphans, or victims of violence.*

4. Martin Luther King Jr.: Leading with Love in the Face of Hatred

Dr. Martin Luther King Jr. is remembered for his leadership in the Civil Rights Movement. He advocated for racial equality and justice, but he did so with a deep commitment to nonviolence and love. His actions were motivated by his Christian faith, and he famously said, "Love is the only force capable of transforming an enemy into a friend."

How You Can Reflect God's Love:

- *Volunteer for community-building activities that encourage understanding and peace.*
- *Be kind to others, even when they disagree with you, and be willing to have respectful conversations about difficult topics.*

5. Albert Schweitzer: Serving Through Medical Missions

Albert Schweitzer was a theologian, philosopher, and physician who spent much of his life in Africa, providing medical care to those in need. His decision to leave his successful career in Europe and dedicate himself to serving the sick in Africa reflected a deep commitment to serving others out of love for Christ.

How You Can Reflect God's Love:

- *Volunteer for medical missions or healthcare initiatives, whether locally or internationally.*

- *Offer to help with the physical or emotional needs of your community.*
- *Advocate for better healthcare access for those who are underserved.*

2. Being a Light in Challenging Environments

Sometimes, the most significant opportunities to reflect God's love come in the most challenging environments. Whether at work, school, or in our families, we will inevitably find ourselves in places where negativity, conflict, or darkness may prevail. Yet, the Bible calls us to be light in these very spaces. Jesus said in Matthew 5:14-16, "You are the light of the world. A town built on a hill cannot be hidden. Neither do people light a lamp and put it under a bowl. Instead, they put it on its stand, and it gives light to everyone in the house. In the same way, let your light shine before others, that they may see your good deeds and glorify your Father in heaven."

Being a light in challenging environments means consistently choosing to reflect Christ's love in the face of difficulty. Here are practical, real-life examples of how you can bring light into dark places:

- **At Work:** *If your workplace is full of gossip or negativity, choose to be the person who encourages others and speaks positively. When faced with difficult situations, be the one who chooses patience, kindness, and integrity.*
- **In Your Family:** *In a home where conflict or stress may be high, choose to be the peacemaker. Offer forgiveness freely, listen patiently, and speak words of encouragement.*
- **In Your Community:** *In a neighborhood where division or tension may exist, be the person who brings people together. Organize a community event, offer a helping hand to a neighbor in need, or just be present to listen.*

Being a light in these environments doesn't require grand gestures; it's about making the decision to reflect Christ's love in even the smallest interactions.

3. Small Acts of Service

While it's easy to think that serving God requires doing something extraordinary, the reality is that the smallest acts of service can make the biggest impact. Jesus Himself modeled this kind of humble service when He washed the feet of His disciples (John 13:12-17). He demonstrated that greatness in the kingdom of God is not about being served but serving others.

Here are 10 small, unique acts of service that anyone can do, no matter where they live:

1. **Write a note of prayer encouragement** *to someone who's going through a tough time.*
2. **Offer to babysit** *for a single parent or a couple who needs a break.*
3. **Shovel snow or mow the lawn** *for an elderly neighbor or someone who is sick.*
4. **Leave a generous tip** *for a waitress or barista, especially when they seem overwhelmed.*
5. **Invite a new person** *in your church or community to lunch or for a walk, making them feel welcomed.*
6. **Call or visit someone** *who is homebound or in a nursing home, just to chat and brighten their day.*
7. **Help a co-worker with a difficult task** *without expecting anything in return.*
8. **Pick up litter** *in your neighborhood or local park, even if it's not your responsibility.*
9. **Send a gift**—*whether a book, a plant, or a handmade item*—*to someone who needs encouragement.*
10. **Support a local small business** *by leaving a positive review or referring others to them.*

These simple, everyday acts of service allow us to love others well and reflect God's love in our actions.

Serving God in everyday life doesn't require us to do something extraordinary—it's about the small, practical ways we reflect His love to those around us. Whether through acts of kindness, being a light in challenging environments, or performing small acts of service, each opportunity is a chance to point others to Christ. The historical figures we've studied, from Mother Teresa to Albert Schweitzer, showed us that living out our faith means meeting people where they are with love and care. We may not always be able to do great things, but we can do small things with great love.

As you go about your daily routine, ask yourself: How can I reflect God's love today? Whether it's through a kind word, a generous action, or simply being a light in a dark place, each moment is an opportunity to serve Him.

Closing Prayer:

Jesus, Thank You for letting us be part of how You love the world. Help this reader walk out of this chapter ready to love big in small ways. And maybe refill the coffee pot at work. To those that like that bitter bean juice, that's kingdom work too. Amen.

Chapter 12: Celebrating the Journey

Opening Prayer:

Lord, We made it! Let this chapter be a spiritual confetti cannon. Help this reader pause, reflect, and see how far they've come. Even if it felt slow or messy—growth happened. Thank You for being faithful every chapter. Amen.

The journey of faith is not about reaching perfection but about embracing progress. Too often, we become so fixated on the idea of "arriving" at a place of complete spiritual success that we overlook the joy and beauty of the journey itself. The truth is, spiritual growth is a process—a journey that includes both victories and setbacks. Along the way, we are called to celebrate progress, not perfection. We are invited to seek forgiveness when we stumble, and to extend grace to ourselves as we continue to grow in our relationship with God. This chapter is all about celebrating that journey, embracing the progress you've made, and finding joy in walking with God every step of the way.

Celebrate Progress, Not Perfection

In a world that often measures success by the ultimate outcome, it's easy to get caught up in the pursuit of perfection. Whether it's our personal achievements, spiritual growth, or the way we live out our faith, we can fall into the trap of thinking that if we're not perfect, we're failing. But the Bible teaches us that the process of growth is just as important as the end result.

Philippians 3:12-14 reminds us of this truth: "Not that I have already obtained all this, or have already arrived at my goal, but I press on to take hold of that for which Christ Jesus took hold of me. Brothers and sisters, I do not consider myself yet to have taken hold of it. But one thing I do: Forgetting what is behind and straining toward what is ahead, I press on toward the goal to win the prize for which God has called me heavenward in Christ Jesus."

Paul's words are a powerful reminder that we are not called to perfection but to perseverance. It's not about having it all together— it's about pressing on, continuing to strive, and moving forward in our walk with God. Each step, even the smallest, is part of the journey, and God celebrates our progress, no matter how slow or imperfect it may seem.

Another verse that underscores this message is 2 Corinthians 5:17, which states, "Therefore, if anyone is in Christ, the new creation has come: The old has gone, the new is here!" The process of spiritual growth means we are continually being transformed, day by day. We are not perfect, but we are being perfected. The old is behind, and with each new day, God's grace is making us new.

Don't Beat Yourself Up: Seek Forgiveness and Give Yourself Grace

As we walk this journey, we will undoubtedly stumble. We will fall short of God's standard. We will sin, we will get discouraged, and we may even feel like giving up. But here's the beautiful truth: our mistakes do not define us. God's grace and forgiveness are always available to us, no matter how many times we fall.

Isaiah 1:18 offers a profound promise of restoration: "Come now, let us settle the matter," says the Lord. "Though your sins are like scarlet, they shall be as white as snow; though they are red as crimson, they shall be like wool." When we make a mistake, we do not need to dwell in shame or guilt. We are invited to come to God, confess, and receive His forgiveness. The beauty of this is that God's love for us is not based on our perfection but on His grace.

Psalm 103:10-12 reminds us of the depth of God's forgiveness: "He does not treat us as our sins deserve or repay us according to our iniquities. For as high as the heavens are above the earth, so great is his love for those who fear him; as far as the east is from the west, so far has he removed our transgressions from us." God's forgiveness is boundless, and His grace is sufficient. There is no sin too great for God to forgive, and no failure too significant for His love to cover.

It is also important to extend grace to ourselves. Often, we are our harshest critics. We may look at our flaws and think we are unworthy of God's love and forgiveness. But the reality is that God has already extended grace to us, and we must learn to do the same. Romans 8:1 declares, "Therefore, there is now no condemnation for those who are in Christ Jesus." You are not condemned, no matter how far you may feel from perfection. God sees you through the lens of His love and grace, and He calls you to do the same.

When you stumble, remember that the journey is not about being flawless. It's about learning, growing, and trusting in God's transforming power. Instead of beating yourself up, seek forgiveness, give yourself grace, and press on toward the goal. God is more concerned with your heart and your willingness to keep walking with Him than with your perfection.

The Joy of Walking with God

One of the most beautiful aspects of the Christian faith is the opportunity to walk with God daily. Walking with God is not just about following rules or checking off boxes on a spiritual to-do list. It's about cultivating an intimate relationship with the Creator of the universe. It's about experiencing His presence, hearing His voice, and allowing His love to shape our lives.

Psalm 16:11 says, "You make known to me the path of life; you will fill me with joy in your presence, with eternal pleasures at your right hand." Walking with God brings joy—not just in the future, but in the present. His presence fills us with a deep, abiding joy that cannot be found in the things of this world. This joy is not dependent on circumstances, but on the unshakable reality of God's love for us.

Jesus said in John 15:9-11, "As the Father has loved me, so have I loved you. Now remain in my love. If you keep my commands, you will remain in my love, just as I have kept my Father's commands and remain in his love. I have told you this so that my joy may be in you and that your joy may be complete." The joy of walking with God comes when we remain in His love. It's not about striving harder or being perfect—it's about staying close to God, trusting in His love, and allowing His joy to fill our hearts.

Walking with God also gives us the strength to face life's challenges with a sense of peace and hope. James 1:2-4 says, "Consider it pure joy, my brothers and sisters, whenever you face trials of many kinds, because you know that the testing of your faith produces perseverance. Let perseverance finish its work so that you may be mature and complete, not lacking anything." Even in the trials, there is joy, because God is using those moments to shape us, grow us, and draw us closer to Him. When we walk with God, we can face life's challenges with hope, knowing that He is with us every step of the way.

An Uplifting Call to Action: Keep Striving, Trusting, and Growing

As you continue on this journey of faith, I encourage you to celebrate the progress you've made. Every step, no matter how small, is a step toward becoming more like Christ. Don't focus on your shortcomings or dwell in regret over past mistakes. Instead, focus on the ways in which God has been faithful to you, and look forward to the ways He will continue to shape you in the future.

I challenge you to take the following tangible goals with you as you move forward:

1. **Set aside time each day for prayer and Bible study.** *This is the foundation of walking with God. It's through these daily practices that we build a deeper relationship with Him.*

2. **Embrace grace when you stumble.** *When you fall short, don't be hard on yourself. Instead, seek God's forgiveness, accept His grace, and keep moving forward.*
3. **Look for opportunities to serve others.** *Serving others is a reflection of God's love. Find small, everyday ways to be a blessing to those around you.*
4. **Celebrate the small victories.** *Take time to recognize the ways you've grown, whether it's in your patience, kindness, or faith. Celebrate your progress, no matter how minor it may seem.*
5. **Trust God with the future.** *Don't worry about what's ahead. Trust that God is with you, guiding you, and that His plans for you are good (Jeremiah 29:11).*
6. **Make joy a priority.** *Walking with God brings joy, so choose to embrace the joy of the journey. Even in hard times, choose to find the joy that comes from being in His presence.*

Remember that the Christian life is not about perfection. It's about progress, grace, and growing closer to God each day. Keep striving, keep trusting, and keep growing. The journey may be long, but the joy of walking with God is worth every step.

"Let us run with perseverance the race marked out for us, fixing our eyes on Jesus, the pioneer and perfecter of faith." (Hebrews 12:1-2)

Conclusion

As we reach the end of this journey, let us pause and reflect on the truths we've explored. Through every chapter, one central theme has stood firm: God's love for you is vast, unshakable, and unconditional. From understanding who God is to embracing His grace and learning to walk faithfully in His light, each step has been a reminder of His desire for a relationship with you—not one built on perfection, but on trust, humility, and love.

God's Love and Grace

"Grace for the Repeat Offender: How God Kept Loving Me Anyway"

Let me be honest—if there were a punch card for sin, mine would be full. And I don't mean "buy nine, get the tenth forgiveness free." I mean I would've needed extra pages stapled to the back. I've sinned so much that at this point, I'm surprised heaven's gates don't have a "do not admit without supervision" sign next to my name.

But here's the wild thing—God? He still came through. He didn't flinch. Didn't throw His hands up in disgust and say, "You know what? I'm out. This one's too much." Nope. He stayed. He loved. And somehow, He got me to today. A little banged up, maybe, but still standing. Mostly.

When I look back at my life, it's like scrolling through a photo album of awkward moments, bad decisions, and seasons I'd rather not repeat. There are chapters where I hurt the people I loved the most, sometimes out of selfishness, sometimes out of pure stupidity. I've hurt myself too—spiritually, emotionally, even physically. And not in some dramatic, rock-bottom-in-the-rain kind of way either. Sometimes the most dangerous damage comes from little choices that wear you down over time—like spiritual paper cuts. You don't think they're serious, until your heart's got Band-Aids on every inch.

There were years I thought I was doing fine. I was "functioning." I had the Christian T-shirts, the bumper sticker, the ability to quote half of Philippians out of context. But my heart? It was wandering. I'd sit in church with a smile on my face and a whole circus going on inside. Guilt, shame, secrets, pride—those were the real Sunday shoes I wore.

And yet, God was faithful.

Not faithful in a "Well, I guess I'll forgive her again" kind of way, but faithful in the "I already knew this would happen, and I still chose you" kind of way. The kind that makes you cry into your orange juice at 6:43 in the morning because He's just that good.

I've started and stopped so many "new me" seasons, I should open a pop-up shop called "This Time It's Different." One minute I'm praying like I'm ready to go full missionary in the Amazon, the next I'm binge-watching nonsense and ignoring God's nudges like He's a bill collector.

But something shifted. Slowly. Like watching bread rise. You don't see the moment it happens, but you come back later and realize it's grown.

I started to understand that being a Christian wasn't about achieving sinless perfection. (Spoiler: not happening.) It's about progress. It's about falling flat on your face, but knowing that the ground you're face-planting on is grace. It's about getting up again—sometimes with mascara running and Cheeto dust on your shirt—and saying, "Okay, Lord. Let's try again."

And He always says, "Let's."

There were times I thought my sins were too big. Not for God to forgive—He's God, after all—but for me to live past. I figured I'd be the cautionary tale in someone's testimony. "Don't be like her, kids." But God doesn't write people off. He rewrites stories. And I know because He rewrote mine. In pen.

He took my anger and slowly turned it into compassion. He took my mistakes and used them to soften my heart instead of harden it. He took all my ridiculous plans and said, "Cute. Now come over here and watch what I can do."

And He was right. Of course He was right.

I used to think the goal of the Christian life was to get better so God would be proud of me. But that's backwards. God doesn't wait for improvement before He loves us. His love is the thing that makes us better. It's like trying to get clean before you take a shower—doesn't make sense.

I'm not where I want to be yet. Not even close. There are still days I act like I've never even heard of Jesus. I still say things I shouldn't, still let fear get the best of me, still eat snacks in bed even though I promised myself I'd stop (okay that one's not a sin, but it feels like one at 2 a.m. when crumbs are involved).

But now, when I mess up, I don't run from God. I run toward Him. Because I've finally realized He's not mad at me—He's for me. He's not shocked by my mess—He's already working in it. He's not tallying up my failures—He's offering fresh mercy with every morning breath.

I think sometimes we confuse conviction with condemnation. But conviction says, "Hey, you're better than this—let's go higher." Condemnation says, "You're the worst. Stay down." And that voice of condemnation? That's not Jesus. That's the enemy trying to convince you that your past defines your future. But Jesus already handled the past. All of it. Every shady decision, every angry word, every poor judgment call made at midnight or on a Monday—He covered it. And He still wants you. Wants me.

I used to think I had to fix myself before I could be useful. Now I know that God does His best work in people who know they can't fix themselves.

He didn't call me because I was good; He called me because He is.

And if He can use me—mistake-prone, overthinking, hot-mess me—then He can use anyone. He's not looking for shiny Christians who always get it right. He's looking for honest hearts that keep coming back.

That's what I'm learning to do. Come back. Again and again. To His Word, to His presence, to His truth when the lies feel louder. I don't always get it right. Sometimes I get it wrong in new, creative ways. But I'm coming back. And I'm growing. And that, my friend, is progress.

So if you're reading this thinking, "I've screwed up too much," let me lovingly tell you: join the club. But don't stay stuck. God already knew about every mistake you'd make—and He still picked you. His love doesn't expire. His grace isn't rationed. And His plan isn't canceled because of detours.

We aren't disqualified. We're in process. It's not always pretty, but it's real. And God honors real. Not performance, not perfection—just real.

So here I am, stumbling forward. Learning to forgive myself. Learning to ask for help. Learning to say, "Lord, I need You," a dozen times a day. And learning to laugh at myself too—because let's be honest, some of these lessons? Hilarious in hindsight.

Like the time I tried to "fast social media" and lasted 42 minutes before logging on to "just check one thing." Or the time I told God I'd be patient if He'd just hurry up and fix everything. (Spoiler: He didn't. But He changed me.)

It's okay to be a work in progress. That's what we are—God's project, still under construction, but built on the firm foundation of Christ. And when He's done? It'll be glorious.

In the meantime, I'll be here—water bottle in one hand, Bible in the other, trying again.

Because He's worth it.

And—somehow—He thinks I'm worth it too.

At the heart of your faith is the truth found in John 3:16: "For God so loved the world, that he gave his only Son, that whoever believes in him should not perish but have eternal life." This love is not reserved for the faultless but is extended to all, even in our brokenness. Romans 8:38-39 assures us, "For I am sure that neither death nor life, nor angels nor rulers, nor things present nor things to come, nor powers, nor height nor depth, nor anything else in all creation, will be able to separate us from the love of God in Christ Jesus our Lord."

Through His grace, you are forgiven, redeemed, and empowered to live fully. Ephesians 2:8-9 reminds us, "For by grace you have been saved through faith. And this is not your own doing; it is the gift of God, not a result of works, so that no one may boast." Embrace this grace, allowing it to transform your heart and guide your actions.

Practical Steps for Growing in Faith
Faith is not confined to grand gestures or perfect performance—it's cultivated through small, consistent acts of devotion. Pray without ceasing (1 Thessalonians 5:17), seek God in your daily moments (Matthew 6:33), and let His Word be a lamp to your feet and a light to your path (Psalm 119:105).

Celebrate the joy of living a life that honors God, knowing that the fullness of joy is found in His presence (Psalm 16:11). Allow His Spirit to guide you in balancing faith and life, reminding you that all good things come from Him (James 1:17).

An Encouraging Call to Action
Though the journey may feel overwhelming at times, remember Philippians 1:6: "He who began a good work in you will bring it to completion at the day of Jesus Christ." Trust in God's process, celebrating the progress you've made rather than focusing on perfection.

As you move forward, take to heart the words of Galatians 6:9: "Let us not grow weary of doing good, for in due season we will reap, if we do not give up." Surround yourself with a supportive community, lean on God in moments of temptation, and let your life be a reflection of His love and grace to those around you.

A Closing Prayer:

Heavenly Father,

Thank You for the reader who has embarked on this journey of faith. Bless them with the courage to grow closer to You daily, the strength to overcome temptation, and the joy of living fully in Your presence. Remind them that they are loved beyond measure and that Your grace is sufficient in all circumstances. Guide their steps, and let Your light shine brightly in their lives, drawing others to You through their example. May they trust in Your plans, rejoice in Your promises, and maybe let them eat cake to celebrate. You're good like that. In Jesus' name, Amen.

Go forth with faith, hope, and love, knowing that

God walks with you every step of the way.

Suggested Reading Plan and Devotionals

This reading plan for Living Fully, Loving God: A Practical Guide for Everyday Faith and is designed to help you grow closer to God, overcome challenges, and live a joyful, faith-filled life. The plan spans 30 days, allowing for reflection and practical application.

Week 1: Understanding God and Ourselves

Day 1-3: *Who Is God?*

- **Scriptures**: *Psalm 103:8-14, Isaiah 40:28-31, Matthew 11:28-30.*
- **Reflection**: *What misconceptions about God might you need to let go of? How can you experience God as loving and personal?*

Day 4-6: *Acknowledging the Struggle*

- **Scriptures**: *Romans 3:23, James 1:13-15, 1 Corinthians 10:13.*
- **Reflection**: *What are the areas where you face temptation? How can you rely on God's strength to face them?*

Day 7: *Grace and Forgiveness*

- **Scriptures**: *Ephesians 2:8-9, Luke 15:11-32, 1 John 1:9.*
- **Reflection**: *Reflect on God's grace in your life. Write a prayer of gratitude for His forgiveness.*

Week 2: Practical Steps to Grow Closer to God

Day 8-10: *Building a Relationship with God*

- **Scriptures**: *Jeremiah 29:12-13, Psalm 145:18, Philippians 4:6-7.*

- **Reflection**: *Try journaling your prayers or spending 10 minutes in silent prayer.*

Day 11-12: *Balancing Faith and Fun*

- **Scriptures**: *John 10:10, Ecclesiastes 3:12-13, 1 Timothy 6:17.*
- **Reflection**: *What activities bring you joy and honor God? Plan a God-centered day of rest and fun.*

Day 13-14: *Daily Habits for Spiritual Growth*

- **Scriptures**: *Colossians 3:16-17, Joshua 1:8, Philippians 2:14-16.*
- **Reflection**: *Commit to a small habit like reading a verse daily or expressing gratitude in prayer.*

Week 3: Overcoming Temptation

Day 15-17: *Identifying Triggers and Patterns*

- **Scriptures**: *Proverbs 4:23, Galatians 5:16-17, Psalm 139:23-24.*
- **Reflection**: *Identify moments when you feel spiritually weak and create a plan to address them.*

Day 18-19: *Strategies for Overcoming Temptation*

- **Scriptures**: *Matthew 4:1-11, 2 Corinthians 10:3-5, 1 Peter 5:8-10.*
- **Reflection**: *Memorize a scripture that strengthens you in moments of weakness.*

Day 20-21: *Community and Support*

- **Scriptures**: *Hebrews 10:24-25, Ecclesiastes 4:9-10, Acts 2:42-47.*
- **Reflection**: *How can you engage more deeply with a supportive faith community?*

Week 4: Living Faithfully Every Day

Day 22-23: *Imperfect but Loved*

- **Scriptures**: *Romans 8:1, 2 Corinthians 12:9-10, Psalm 34:18.*
- **Reflection**: *Reflect on biblical figures who were imperfect yet loved and used by God.*

Day 24-25: *Serving God in Everyday Life*

- **Scriptures**: *Matthew 5:14-16, Galatians 5:13, Micah 6:8.*
- **Reflection**: *Plan one small act of kindness or service to reflect God's love today.*

Day 26-27: *Celebrating the Journey*

- **Scriptures**: *Philippians 3:12-14, Psalm 100:4-5, Nehemiah 8:10.*
- **Reflection**: *Celebrate your growth and thank God for the steps you've taken.*

Day 28-30: *Revisiting God's Love and Grace*

- **Scriptures**: *Romans 5:8, 1 John 4:16-18, Lamentations 3:22-23.*
- **Reflection**: *Write a prayer or journal entry celebrating God's faithfulness throughout this journey.*

Here are **12 bonus journaling prompts** *tied to the themes and suggested reading plan from Living Fully, Loving God: A Practical Guide for Everyday Faith.*

1. Who Is God to You? (Chapter 1)

- *Reflect on your current perception of God. Does it align with the idea of a loving, forgiving, and personal God?*
    - *Scripture Tie-In: Read Psalm 103:8–10 and write about how God's compassion and forgiveness impact your view of Him.*

2. Acknowledging the Struggle (Chapter 2)

- *Identify one area where you feel you're struggling with sin or temptation. What feelings or patterns contribute to this struggle?*
    - *Scripture Tie-In: Read 1 Corinthians 10:13 and write about how God's promise of a way out can bring you hope.*

3. Experiencing Grace and Forgiveness (Chapter 3)

- *Write about a time when you felt unworthy of God's love but experienced His grace. How did it change your perspective?*
    - *Scripture Tie-In: Reflect on Ephesians 2:8–9 and journal about how grace has played a role in your life.*

4. Building a Relationship with God (Chapter 4)

- *Describe your current prayer habits. How can you make them more authentic and personal?*
    - *Scripture Tie-In: After reading Philippians 4:6–7, write about how you can bring all your anxieties and joys to God in prayer.*

5. Balancing Faith and Fun (Chapter 5)

- *What activities bring you joy? How can you incorporate God into these moments to honor Him?*
    - *Scripture Tie-In: Read Ecclesiastes 3:12–13 and reflect on how God intends for us to find enjoyment in life.*

6. Developing Daily Habits for Growth (Chapter 6)

- *List three small habits you can adopt to grow spiritually. How will you hold yourself accountable?*
    - *Scripture Tie-In: Reflect on Psalm 1:2–3 and journal about how meditating on God's Word can nourish your faith.*

7. Identifying Your Triggers (Chapter 7)

- *Write about a specific situation where you felt tempted. What patterns or triggers can you identify?*
    - *Scripture Tie-In: Read James 1:14–15 and consider how understanding the root of temptation can help you avoid it.*

8. Overcoming Temptation (Chapter 8)

- *What strategies have worked for you in resisting temptation? Which areas still need growth?*
    - *Scripture Tie-In: Reflect on Matthew 26:41 and write about how prayer and vigilance can strengthen your resolve.*

9. Finding Community and Support (Chapter 9)

- *Who in your life helps you stay focused on your faith? How can you strengthen those connections?*

- Scripture Tie-In: After reading Hebrews 10:24–25, journal about the value of being part of a faith community.

10. Embracing Imperfection (Chapter 10)

- *Think about a biblical figure who overcame struggles (e.g., David, Peter). How does their story encourage you?*
  - *Scripture Tie-In: Reflect on 2 Corinthians 12:9 and journal about how God's strength is made perfect in your weakness.*

11. Reflecting God's Love in Daily Actions (Chapter 11)

- *Write about an act of kindness you performed recently. How did it reflect God's love?*
  - *Scripture Tie-In: After reading Matthew 5:16, journal about how your actions can glorify God.*

12. Celebrating the Journey (Chapter 12)

- *Reflect on how far you've come in your spiritual journey. What progress can you celebrate today?*
  - *Scripture Tie-In: Read Philippians 1:6 and write about the confidence you have in God's work in your life.*

Scriptures for Strength

Genesis

1. *Genesis 28:15 – "I am with you and will watch over you wherever you go."*
2. *Genesis 31:3 – "Go back to the land of your fathers and to your relatives, and I will be with you."*

Exodus

3. *Exodus 14:14 – "The Lord will fight for you; you need only to be still."*
4. *Exodus 15:2 – "The Lord is my strength and my defense; He has become my salvation."*

Deuteronomy

5. *Deuteronomy 1:30 – "The Lord your God, who is going before you, will fight for you."*
6. *Deuteronomy 20:4 – "For the Lord your God is the one who goes with you to fight for you."*
7. *Deuteronomy 31:6 – "Be strong and courageous. Do not be afraid or terrified because of them."*
8. *Deuteronomy 31:8 – "The Lord Himself goes before you and will be with you."*

Joshua

9. *Joshua 1:5 – "No one will be able to stand against you all the days of your life."*
10. *Joshua 1:9 – "Be strong and courageous. Do not be afraid; do not be discouraged, for the Lord your God will be with you wherever you go."*

Psalms

11. *Psalm 18:2 – "The Lord is my rock, my fortress, and my deliverer."*
12. *Psalm 18:32 – "It is God who arms me with strength and keeps my way secure."*
13. *Psalm 23:4 – "Even though I walk through the darkest valley, I will fear no evil."*
14. *Psalm 27:1 – "The Lord is my light and my salvation—whom shall I fear?"*
15. *Psalm 29:11 – "The Lord gives strength to His people; the Lord blesses His people with peace."*
16. *Psalm 34:17 – "The righteous cry out, and the Lord hears them; He delivers them from all their troubles."*
17. *Psalm 46:1 – "God is our refuge and strength, an ever-present help in trouble."*
18. *Psalm 55:22 – "Cast your cares on the Lord and He will sustain you."*
19. *Psalm 73:26 – "My flesh and my heart may fail, but God is the strength of my heart and my portion forever."*
20. *Psalm 118:14 – "The Lord is my strength and my defense; He has become my salvation."*

Isaiah
21. *Isaiah 12:2 – "Surely God is my salvation; I will trust and not be afraid."*
22. *Isaiah 40:29-31 – "He gives strength to the weary and increases the power of the weak."*
23. *Isaiah 41:10 – "Do not fear, for I am with you."*
24. *Isaiah 41:13 – "I am the Lord your God who takes hold of your right hand."*
25. *Isaiah 43:2 – "When you pass through the waters, I will be with you."*

Philippians

26. *Philippians 4:13 – "I can do all things through Christ who strengthens me."*

Romans

27. *Romans 8:31 – "If God is for us, who can be against us?"*

2 Corinthians

28. *2 Corinthians 12:9 – "My grace is sufficient for you, for my power is made perfect in weakness."*

Scriptures for Encouragement

John

29. *John 14:27 – "Peace I leave with you; my peace I give you."*

30. *John 16:33 – "In this world you will have trouble. But take heart! I have overcome the world."*

Matthew

31. *Matthew 11:28-30 – "Come to me, all you who are weary and burdened, and I will give you rest."*

Psalms

32. *Psalm 23:1-4 – "The Lord is my shepherd; I lack nothing."*

33. *Psalm 37:4 – "Take delight in the Lord, and He will give you the desires of your heart."*

34. *Psalm 42:11 – "Why, my soul, are you downcast? Put your hope in God."*

Proverbs

35. *Proverbs 3:5-6 – "Trust in the Lord with all your heart."*

Isaiah

36. *Isaiah 41:13 – "For I am the Lord your God who takes hold of your right hand."*

Romans

37. *Romans 8:28 – "We know that in all things God works for the good of those who love Him."*

Scriptures for Overcoming Temptation

1 Corinthians

38. *1 Corinthians 10:13 – "No temptation has overtaken you except what is common to mankind."*

James

39. *James 1:12 – "Blessed is the one who perseveres under trial."*
40. *James 4:7 – "Submit yourselves, then, to God. Resist the devil, and he will flee from you."*

Matthew

41. *Matthew 4:4 – "Man shall not live on bread alone."*
42. *Matthew 26:41 – "Watch and pray so that you will not fall into temptation."*

Galatians

43. *Galatians 5:16 – "Walk by the Spirit, and you will not gratify the desires of the flesh."*

Psalms

44. *Psalm 119:11 – "I have hidden Your word in my heart that I might not sin against You."*

Made in the USA
Columbia, SC
30 June 2025